FINISHED WORK of CHRIST

GROUP STUDY WORKBOOK

WENDY J. CLARK

ISBN: 978-1-7354954-5-3

All scripture references from NKJV unless otherwise quoted
Copyright © 1982 by Thomas Nelson. Used by permission. All rights reserved.
All Greek and Hebrew references used in whole or in part are from
Strong's Concordance & Strong's Exhaustive Concordance.
Other resources used are indicated by the key below:
† Helps Word-Studies
‡ NAS Exhaustive Concordance
§ Brown-Driver-Briggs
# NASB Translation
* Thayer's Greek Lexicon
** Dictionary.com Unabridged
†† Merriam-Webster Dictionary

Thanks to Biblehub.com and BibleGateway.com
for providing such great Online tools to study the Word of God.

SWORD OF THE SPIRIT & POWER OF THE TONGUE
SPEAK IT®

For my Lord and Savior,

You plucked me out of corruption,
restored me and set me on high.
In your light, I'm continually changed,
and perpetually overcome by your love.

Herein is love, not that we loved God, but that he loved us,
and sent his Son to be the propitiation for our sins.

1 JOHN 4:10

CONTENTS

ENDORSEMENTS

This book is such good news! What a privilege to recommend to you this treasure of truth. It will warm your heart and establish your mindset completely in the love of God revealed to each of us in the Finished Work of Christ. Wendy has a great gift in providing nuggets of revelation that will reinforce in you the beauty of believing, and establish your faith in what God in Christ has done for you. This book is perfect for personal devotions or group study. We know you will experience the hope and grace Jesus provides as you are ever conscious of 'The Finishe• Work Of Christ' in your daily life. Enjoy.

KEITH & HEIDI HERSHEY
FOUNDERS; MUTUAL FAITH MINISTRIES INTERNATIONAL

Many today want to accomplish the goal of reading through the Bible in one year, but Bible reading isn't about achieving goals, it's a lifetime journey. The real goal is never to stop learning, meditating, and being willing to let our eyes be opened. The time to start is now, and Wendy's new book is filled with remarkable research that will open the Bible in a way you've never experienced it before.

KATHLEEN COOKE
CO-FOUNDER OF COOKE MEDIA GROUP AND THE INFLUENCE LAB
AUTHOR OF HOPE 4 TODAY: STAY CONNECTED TO GOD IN A
DISTRACTED CULTURE.

The Finishe• Work of Christ is full of every promise that will lead you to the revelation of not just believing that "it is finished" but *knowing* that IT IS FINISHED! After reading this book you will never doubt the true nature of God again. Wendy writes her *Speak It®* books based on the truth and meaning of the scriptures. They contain all the information we need to cross reference book by book in the Bible, and through the Greek and Hebrew. The result is that we know exactly what was meant and how much authority we carry as born again, Jesus-loving Christians. This book is not based on human opinion or human experience—NO! It is based on truth—the truth that sets you free!

JULIEANN HARTMAN
HEALING JOURNEYS TODAY

IT'S A BIBLE STUDY WITHIN A BIBLE STUDY...

Because I know the author, I know this: What you are about to read is a labor of love and the result of personal study, application, revelation and realization of the living Word of God. This book is a wonderful invitation to dig deep in the Scripture to explore and solidify the foundation of our life in Christ. As Wendy puts it, "We will keep ourselves in the middle of His amazing love, and receive tremendous, never-ending revelation of it, by keeping our eyes fixed on His mercy that was poured out through the Finished Work (Jude 20-21)."

DEBRA ARNOTT
DEAN OF KINGDOM MOVEMENT SCHOOL OF MINISTRY

To the Believer

Whether you've been in Christ for 40 days or 40 years, to extract every ounce of manna from this book it's essential to resist the thought, "I already know this." A common tendency of us all in Christ, this is not our thought. It's a lofty argument from the enemy attempting to undermine the continual maturing of our relationship with God. It is designed to hinder us from drawing from the never-ending wells of salvation and receiving perpetual revelation of *the* foundational message of our faith.

We all have taken on preconceived ideas about scripture. But I encourage you to come to this text with child-like eyes and a humble heart to let the word of God enlighten your understanding. This posture will allow the Holy Spirit to bring you into a deeper revelation of the Finished Work of Christ.

Having clarity of understanding we will access all He provided. We'll not only be secure in our eternal salvation, but we'll be able to live victoriously and walk in His provision and power.

The purpose of this book is to emphasize sound doctrine. It will bring cohesion to the central teachings of scripture and associate themes that previously seemed unconnected. It will open the eyes of our understanding to things that were previously veiled, and flood our hearts with revelation light. It will fortify our Christian walk on foundational truths that were established before the beginning of creation. We will read the Bible and unlock its treasure as clarity of understanding pours forth through the very breath of God.

Essential-Read This First

We could meditate on His Finished Work until He returned and never get to the end of it. The more understanding we receive, the more we'll take hold of all He accomplished for us at Calvary.

After all, He emphatically assured us, **whoever believes in Him** will do the works He did, and even greater, because He ascended to the Father (John 14:12). He expects us to carry on His miracle ministry **to the ends of the earth** (Acts 1:8). As we read, we should expect to walk in these greater works.

> "Truly, truly, I say to you, **he who believes in Me,** the works that I do, he will do also; and greater works than these he will do; because I go to the Father. JOHN 14:12 NASB 1995
>
> But you shall receive power when the Holy Spirit has come upon you; and you shall be witnesses to Me in Jerusalem, and in all Judea and Samaria, and **to the end of the earth."** ACTS 1:8

As any work from Speak It,® *The Finished Work of Christ* is a deep biblical study tool. Allow these truths to sink into your heart as you meditate in fellowship with the Holy Spirit. By it, your eyes will be opened to the unfathomable depths of His love. It will forever change your heart and empower your walk.

NEW CREATION REALITY

To properly develop New Creation thinking, it is essential to know how to apply Old Testament scriptures to the reality of the Finished Work of Christ. Therefore, we expound Old Testament scriptures concerning Jesus from the perspective of this side of the Cross.

BUILDING SOLID DOCTRINE FOLLOWING THE TRAIL

To simplify complex subjects, tie them together and build in understanding is key. To link scriptures and word definitions to the devotional text, there are numerical references throughout.

A superscript number in the devotional text, for example, "the prayer of faith ministered by an *elder,³"* points to the same number in a scripture box, or a key Greek or Hebrew word box, sometimes both. This make linking ideas from the devotional text back to the scriptures easy to pinpoint and compare.

> Is anyone among you sick? Let him call for the *elders³* of the church... **JAMES 5:14**

> **KEY GREEK WORD**
> **4245 PRESBUTEROS:³**
> (pres-boo'-ter-os) elder...

These superscript numbers can appear several times within one chapter, so keep your eyes open and follow the numeric trail—some chapters have a little more complexity than others. Take the time to read each scripture and each definition. In doing so, connections will be made, and deeper meanings will become apparent that solidify your understanding.

There is so much depth in each chapter, it's important to read, and re-read. Each time, you'll see things you didn't see before, as the Holy Spirit reveals more and more to you individually.

As we determine to know nothing but *Christ and Him crucified,* we too will walk in demonstration of His power. Our faith, and the faith of those around us, will be in Him (1 Corinthians 2:2-5)!

> For I determined not to know anything among you except *Jesus Christ and Him crucified.* I was with you in weakness, in fear, and in much trembling. And my speech and my preaching were not with persuasive words of human wisdom, *but in demonstration of the Spirit and of power,* that your faith should not be in the wisdom of men but in the power of God. **1 CORINTHIANS 2:2-5**

Study Focus Points

Wherever you see the following graphic icons pause and reflect. They highlight some important points to take special note of.

👣 FOUNDATIONAL FOOTPRINT

This is a fundamental doctrinal truth that needs to be clearly understood to have the correct foundational knowledge of all scripture.

💧 SATURATION POINT

Meditate on this until it drops into your spirit as a revelation. Don't be quick to move on from here—really focus and soak this one in.

❶ THE LAW OF FIRST MENTION

The very first time a subject is mentioned in the Bible it should be recognized as *the* most important, foundational truth about that subject. It serves as the key to understanding the fundamental and inherent meaning of that subject throughout scripture.

🄰 SHADOWS AND TYPES

God speaks to us in pictures. In fact, the whole Bible is full of shadows and types, which are (mostly) pictures of Jesus and His Finished Work. The picture is the *shadow and type* and the *substance (antitype)* is the fulfillment in Jesus. When the Holy Spirit enlightens the picture in a flash of revelation understanding, true biblical faith arises. Then we automatically speak and act from faith, and His power is released into our situation.

⌐O KEY CONCEPTS FOR GREEK GRAMMAR

It's essential to study the original text in the Greek and Hebrew to properly understand scripture. Because the English doesn't have as much specificity of grammatical separation as other languages, it can lose some meaning in the translation, especially some of the looser, modern Bible translations which are more like Bible interpretations. The King James Version is one of the closest to the original text. Even so, biblical Greek is difficult to misinterpret, and when we examine the original text, we can still draw out much clearer and deeper insight.

To properly translate and interpret the correct meaning from the original text it's important to study an interlinear Bible that reads from the original Greek or Hebrew, rather than one that reads from English.

We study word definitions and analyze form and punctuation of sentences. When you observe the root combinations that form individual words, the Koine Greek has especially rich understanding to uncover.

The Septuagint, which is the Old Testament translated into Koine Greek, is another tool that is helpful to understand how first century Christians interpreted the Hebrew.

GREEK VERBS

Use this tool as a reference to understand the form of the Greek verbs. Depending on their aspect they change the context and meaning. The basic aspects are person, number, voice, mood and tense.

PERSON *The subject of the verb*

FIRST PERSON The person *speaking* is the subject of the action, "*I* live."

SECOND PERSON The person being *spoken to* is the subject of the action, "*You* live."

THIRD PERSON The person being *spoken about* is the subject of the action, "*He* lives"

NUMBER *Singular or plural*

VOICE *Who is ●oing the action*

ACTIVE The subject is performing the action, e.g. *Jesus* was baptizing.

PASSIVE The subject is being acted upon or is the recipient of the action, e.g. *Jesus* was baptized by John in the Jordan.

MIDDLE The subject is performing the action acting upon himself, e.g. *I* am washing myself.

MOOD

Mood deals with whether the statement is actual fact or only a possibility. If the sentence is being stated as a fact, the mood reflects this regardless of whether it is true or false. **INDICATIVE** is the only mood conceived of as actual fact. In the other three moods, the action is thought of as possible or potential.

INDICATIVE A statement of fact or an actual occurrence from the writer's or speaker's perspective, e.g. "And they *overcame* him by the blood of the Lamb... (Revelation 12:11)."

IMPERATIVE A command or instruction charging the hearer to perform a certain action, e.g. "*Flee* youthful lusts (2 Timothy 2:22)."

SUBJUNCTIVE Indicates probability or possibility—the action of the verb *will possibly happen* depending on certain factors or circumstances. It is often used in conditional statements, i.e. if/then clauses.

However, if the subjunctive mood is used on a verb in a purpose or result clause, then the action should not be thought of as a possible result but as a definite outcome, e.g. "In order that now the manifold wisdom of God might be *ma●e known* through the church... (Ephesians 3:10)."

OPTATIVE The mood of possibility is removed even further than the subjunctive. Often used to convey a wish or hope for a certain action to occur, e.g. "And the very God of peace sanctify you wholly; and I *pray* God your whole spirit and soul and body be preserved blameless unto the coming of our Lord Jesus Christ (1 Thessalonians 5:23)."

TENSE

In most languages the tense of a verb refers to the **TIME OF THE ACTION** —present, past, or future. But in Greek, the primary consideration is the **KIND OF ACTION** that the verb portrays, and time is secondary.

The **KIND OF ACTION** will fall into one of three categories:

1. **CONTINUOUS** Progressive.
2. **COMPLETED** Accomplished with continuing results.
3. **SIMPLE** Summary or punctiliar occurrence without reference to progress. Simple doesn't always imply the action only happened at one point of time, but it is dependent on the meaning of the verb and other words in the context.

The only place in which the **TIME OF THE ACTION** comes to bear directly upon the tense of a verb is in the indicative mood. In all other moods the **KIND OF ACTION** is primary.

PRESENT Usually denotes continuous action in progress or a state of persistence. In the indicative mood, present tense denotes action going on in the present time, e.g. "In Whom you also *are being built* together into a dwelling place of God in spirit (Ephesians 2:22)."

AORIST Simple or summary occurrence without regard for the amount of time taken. Often referred to as punctiliar (single, one point-in-time action) although it may actually take place over a period of time. In the indicative mood, aorist tense denotes action that occurred in the past, and is often translated like the English simple past tense, e.g. "God... *made us alive together with* Christ (Ephesians 2:5)."

IMPERFECT Shows linear type of action going on for some extended period of time, continually or repeatedly in the past, e.g. "And with many such parables *He spoke (He kept speaking)* the word to them as they were able to hear it (Mark 4:33)." However, when the verb 1510 EIMÍ "to be" is in the imperfect tense it should be considered a simple action happening in past time, e.g. "For *you were* once darkness, but now light in the Lord (Ephesians 5:8)."

PERFECT Unlike the English perfect tense which indicates a completed past action, the Greek perfect tense indicates an action that has been completed and the finished results are now in existence, continuing on in full effect. For example, Galatians 2:20 should be translated "I am in a present state of having been crucified with Christ," indicating that not only was I crucified with Christ in the past, but I am existing now in that present condition.

FUTURE Just like the English future tense—an anticipated action or a certain happening that will occur in the future, e.g. "We know that if he is manifested, *we will be* like Him, for *we will see* Him even as He is (1 John 3:2)."

PLUPERFECT Past perfect shows action that is complete and existed at some time in the past indicated by the context. This tense is only found in the indicative mood and is rarely used in the New Testament, e.g. "All the angels *stoo*ᵥ around the throne and the elders and the four living creatures, and fell on their faces before the throne and worshiped God,... (Revelation 7:11)."

FUTURE PERFECT Much like pluperfect only the completed state will exist at some time in the future. Very rarely used in the New Testament. "And I will give you the keys of the kingdom of heaven, and whatever you bind on earth will *be boun*ᵥ in heaven, and whatever you loose on earth will *be loose*ᵥ in heaven (Matthew 16:19)."

GREEK NOUNS

NOMINATIVE The subject of the verb, *"He* went"

VOCATIVE The person(s) being directly addressed, "Jesus spoke to *him.*"

ACCUSATIVE The direct object of the verb, "They cast their *nets.*"

GENITIVE The one possessing the noun, *"His* Word."

DATIVE The indirect object, instrument, or location, "Go to the *temple.*"

Key Concepts for Greek Grammar has been edited and used by permission ©New Creation Life Intl.

The Foundation of the Word

> *In the beginning was the Word,[1]* and the Word was with God, and the Word was God. He was in the beginning with God. All things were made through Him, and without Him nothing was made that was made. *In Him was life, and the life was the light of men.[2]* And the light shines in the darkness, and the darkness did not comprehend it. JOHN 1:1-5

Jesus *is the Word[1]* (John 1:1-5).  From Genesis to Revelation, the whole Bible is about Him and His sacrifice to bring us back into intimate relationship with God the Father. Everything we are in the New Covenant is the result of Calvary, and the whole kingdom of God stands on its foundations.

A life that displays evidence of the power of God is a result of having correct doctrinal knowledge and *revelation[2]* understanding of *the* foundational message of the New Covenant. *This revelation is the light that gives us life![2]*

Our continual expanding *revelation[2] of the Finished Work of Christ is* the *rock that the church is being built upon.[3]* These are the *keys of the kingdom[4]* of heaven that give us bold access to all He has accomplished for us.

> Jesus answered and said to him, "Blessed are you, Simon Bar-Jonah, for flesh and blood has not *revealed[2]* this to you, but My Father who is in heaven. And I also say to you that you are Peter, and *on this rock I will build My church,[3]* and the gates of Hades shall not prevail against it. MATTHEW 16:17-18

1

Death and lack are **bound.**[5] Our eternal inheritance is **loosed.**[6] With the keys we stand immovable on grace ground, and through **revelation**[2] we walk through the door that was previously locked from the fall of mankind (Matthew 16:17-19).

> And I will give you **the keys of the kingdom of heaven,**[4] and whatever you **bind**[5] on earth will be bound in heaven, and whatever you **loose**[6] on earth will be loosed in heaven." MATTHEW 16:19
>
> Now all things are of God, who has reconciled us to Himself through Jesus Christ, and has given us the **ministry of reconciliation**[7] 2 CORINTHIANS 5:18

Now, as witnesses (through spiritual eyes) to the death, burial and resurrection of Christ we must carry out the **ministry of reconciliation**[7] that Jesus began and entrusted to us (2 Corinthians 5:18).

> And I, brethren, when I came to you, did not come with excellence of speech or of wisdom declaring to you the testimony of God. For **I determined not to know anything among you except Jesus Christ and Him crucified.**[8] I was with you in weakness, in fear, and in much trembling. And my speech and my preaching were not with persuasive words of human wisdom, **but in demonstration of the Spirit and of power,**[9] that your faith should not be in the wisdom of men but in the power of God. 1 CORINTHIANS 2:1-5
>
> But even if we, or an angel from heaven, preach **any other gospel**[10] to you than what we have preached to you, let him be accursed. GALATIANS 1:8

Like Paul, we must **determine to know and speak nothing of ourselves**[8] or from our own natural understanding. Instead, we preach only what we **perceive in fellowship**[2] with the Holy Spirit, which is always interconnected with some aspect of **Christ and Him crucified.**[8] This is how God's **power**[9] and His kingdom is demonstrated here on earth (1 Corinthians 2:1-5).

💧 Absolutely everything we preach should relate to, be rooted in, and refer back to **the Finished Work of Christ.**[8] If it doesn't, **it's not the gospel**[10] (Galatians 1:8). For this reason, let us give ourselves completely to it.

ABSORBING DEEPER

1/ What is the one main subject of the Bible?

_____

2/ What are shadows and types (see pVI)? What is the substance?

_____

_____

_____

3/ What do we need to be able to see the power of God in our lives?

_____

_____

4/ According to John 1:1-5, what is the biblical definition of light?
In contrast, what is darkness?

_____

_____

_____

5/ What is the rock from Matthew 16:17-18?

_____

_____

6/ What are the keys of the Kingdom and what do they open?

_____

_____

7/ According to Paul, how is the power of God demonstrated?

_____

_____

CHAPTER ONE

THE PURPOSE OF THE FINISHED WORK

> … for this purpose the Son of God was manifested, that He might destroy the works of the devil. **1 JOHN 3:8**

Jesus came to destroy all the works of the devil (1 John 3:8). But what precisely are those works? The devil exalted himself above God's Word to deceive Adam into sinning, thereby breaking his fellowship with God. All corruption that came from the **curse**[1] which was pronounced on mankind and the earth because of the disobedience of Adam is the oppression of the devil (Genesis 3:17-19, Romans 5:12).

Instead of being in perfect Spirit-to-spirit relationship with God and being anointed to be fruitful and multiply, **we fell along with Adam.**[2]

> And unto Adam he said, Because thou hast hearkened unto the voice of thy wife, and hast eaten of the tree, of which I commanded thee, saying, Thou shalt not eat of it: **cursed**[1] is the ground for thy sake; in sorrow shalt thou eat of it all the days of thy life; Thorns also and thistles shall it bring forth to thee; and thou shalt eat the herb of the field; In the sweat of thy face shalt thou eat bread, till thou return unto the ground; for out of it wast thou taken: for dust thou art, and unto dust shalt thou return. **GENESIS 3:17-19 KJV**
>
> Therefore, just as **through one man sin entered the world,**[2] and **death through sin,**[3] and thus death spread to all men, because all sinned— **ROMANS 5:12**

From a creation made in God's image, consumed by His life and light, mankind became a corrupt creation spiritually separated from God. Now with a Spirit-to-soul standing, we were completely overtaken by *sin and death.*[3]

❶ The entire *fall*[2] of man came about because Adam and Eve *fell*[2] for the *subtle guile*[4] of the serpent to deceive. He succeeded in getting them to doubt the Word of God, and instead, they put their faith in his lies (Chapter 2, Genesis 3:1 and Genesis 3:4).

> Now the serpent was more *subtil*[4] than any beast of the field which the Lord God had made. And he said unto the woman, Yea, hath God said, Ye shall not eat of every tree of the garden? **GENESIS 3:1 KJV**

> And the serpent said unto the woman, Ye shall not surely die: **GENESIS 3:4 KJV**

Proving the law of first mention, the devil's main MO has not ceased. Using an endless *myriad of subtleties,*[4] he is relentlessly at work tempting all of us to doubt the Word, specifically, to doubt the Finished Work of Christ and all He provided through it.

When we *fall*[2] for his tactics, we too have essentially put more faith in the word of the devil over the Word of God.

> Therefore submit to God. Resist the devil and he will flee from you. **JAMES 4:7**

If we are to become mature Christians able to take hold of our inheritance here and now, it is essential that we learn resist the devil by truly submitting ourselves to the truth of the Word of God (James 4:7). Clearly, we must know what the Word says about our daily life and its intricate circumstances. This is the only way we will stop *falling*[2] for his never-ending attempts to keep us living *fallen from grace*[2] and subject to the curse (Galatians 5:4 and Chapters 2 and 4).

> You have become estranged from Christ, you who attempt to be justified by law; you have *fallen from grace.*[2] **GALATIANS 5:4**

casting down arguments and every high thing that exalts itself against the knowledge of God, bringing every thought into captivity **to the obedience of Christ,**[5] **2 CORINTHIANS 10:5**

For as by one man's disobedience many were made sinners, so also **by one Man's obedience**[5] many will be made righteous. **ROMANS 5:19**

Every believer must become expertly sensitive to his tactics in order to take every thought captive **to Christ's perfect obedience,**[5] not ours. Certainly, if anything is hinged on our obedience, it will fail (2 Corinthians 10:5, Romans 5:19 and Chapter 5).

Only in the maturity of fully comprehending grace by faith will we walk in the fullness of the power of the New Creation that was made possible by Jesus' Finished Work.

ABSORBING DEEPER

1/ What is the purpose of the Finished Work?

_____

_____

_____

2/ What are the works of the devil?

_____

_____

_____

3/ What kind of creation were we before the fall and what were we consumed by?

_____

_____

_____

_____

4/ What kind of creation did we become because of the fall?

_____

_____

_____

_____

5/ What is the devil's main MO?

_____

_____

REFLECT AND DISCUSS

6/ How will we become mature in Christ?

_____

_____

_____

_____

_____

_____

7/ Do you recognize tactics the enemy has used against you? List two ways you have believed the devil's report over the Word of God.

_____

_____

_____

_____

_____

_____

_____

8/ Find two scriptures for each that declare God's truth over the lie.

_____

_____

_____

_____

_____

_____

_____

CHAPTER TWO

From Original Design to the Fall of Man

> So **God created man in His own image;¹** in the image of God He created him; male and female He created them. Then God blessed them, and God said to them, "Be fruitful and multiply; fill the earth and subdue it; have dominion over the fish of the sea, over the birds of the air, and over every living thing that moves on the earth." **GENESIS 1:27-28**

In order to even begin to understand what Christ did for us and why, we need a clear picture of what Adam had before the fall (Genesis 1:27-28). In perceiving who we were created to be, we will be more able to cooperate with the renewing of our minds to the truth and power of the New Creation man.

THE INTIMACY OF RELATIONSHIP WITH GOD

Formed from the mere dust of the earth, Adam was created a 3-part being; he was *a spirit man who possessed a soul and lived in a body*. Adam opened his eyes in the midst of a *heavenly kiss²* from God (Genesis 2:7). He was not only breathed to life by the creator of heaven and earth, but he was *created in His very image¹* (Genesis 1:27-28). He had perfect Spirit-to-spirit relationship with Him, being *intimately acquainted* from the moment of his creation.

> And the Lord God formed man of the dust of the ground, and *breathed into his nostrils the breath of life;²* and man became a living soul. **GENESIS 2:7 KJV**

> And they heard the sound of the Lord God walking in the garden in the *cool [afternoon breeze] of the day*,[3] ... GENESIS 3:8 AMP

KEY HEBREW WORDS

7307 RUACH:[3] (roo'-akh) breath, wind, *spirit*.

5849 ATAR:[4] (aw-tar') to surround, encircle (for protection).

> What is man that You are mindful of him, and the son of man that You visit him? For You have made him a little lower than the angels, and *You have crowned*[4] *him with glory and honor.* PSALM 8:4-5

Seeing the world from the divine perspective was automatic for Adam, in fact he knew nothing else. He fellowshipped with God *in the evening breeze*,[3] rather he walked with God *in the Spirit.*[3]

Adam was literally *clothed*[4] *in the glory* of God (Psalm 8:4-5)—the Holy Spirit, who is the effectual power of God. He knew only goodness, blessing and the perfection of God's creation. He had *no concept* of death having been created an eternal being. He had free will and autonomy of choice. He was anointed to be fruitful and to multiply, and was given dominion over the entire earth (Genesis 1:27-28).

THE FIRST MENTION OF THE DEVIL

❶ The introduction of the devil (serpent) declares his foremost characteristic—*he is subtle.* This is *the* most important thing we need to understand about his warfare against us. His tactics are cunning, deceitful and difficult to detect. In Genesis 3:1, the serpent posed a question about what God had said that caused Eve to recount His words incorrectly. What

> Now *the serpent was more subtil* than any beast of the field which the Lord God had made. And he said unto the woman, Yea, hath God said, Ye shall not eat of every tree of the garden? GENESIS 3:1

followed next led to the entire fall of mankind. To say the least, becoming experts at identifying the devil's constant subtle deception is essential.

Surrounded by abundance and blessing, Adam and Eve were presented with a choice. Leaving God out of the conversation entirely, tragically, they chose to *put more faith in the word of the serpent*[7] *over the Word of God,*[5] and they ate of the only tree that God had forbidden (Genesis 2:16-17, Genesis 3:4).

And the Lord God **commanded the man, saying,**[5] "Of every tree of the garden you may freely eat; but of the tree of the knowledge of good and evil you shall not eat, for in the day that you eat of it you shall **surely**[6] **die.**[6]"
GENESIS 2:16-17

And the serpent said[7] unto the woman, Ye shall not **surely**[6] **die.**[6] **GENESIS 3:4 KJV**

KEY HEBREW WORD

4191 MUTH:[6] (mooth) to die
In **GENESIS 2:17, H4191 MUTH,** is repeated twice—two deaths.

This is the exact same choice we are faced with *daily*. Will we believe **the Word of God**[5] that declares our provision, health, protection and blessing when we become children of God in Christ? Or will we believe the fears attached to natural circumstances that are designed to cause us to **fall from grace** yet again (Chapters 1 and 4)? Will we walk by faith, or by sight (2 Corinthians 5:7)?

❶ Highlighting and underlining the characteristics of the first mention of the devil in order to learn his strategies is paramount! We see that **with cunning subtlety he deceived Adam and Eve into doubting God's Word,**[7] and he succeeded in getting them to believe his word instead.

This is, and will always be, the devil's main MO against us—**with subtle deception that is difficult to detect, he tempts us to doubt the Word of God.**[7] Over and over again, using every opportune situation, he exploits our weaknesses and chips away at our faith. The only thing that enables us to resist every attack is to continually **submit our attention to God**[8] to receive revelation from the Holy Spirit of the Finished Work of Christ (James 4:7).

For we walk by faith, not by sight.
2 CORINTHIANS 5:7

Therefore **submit to God.**[8] Resist the devil and he will flee from you.
JAMES 4:7

THE PRONOUNCEMENT OF THE CURSE

Reading Genesis 2:17 in the Hebrew, we see the word 4191 MUTH,[6] to die, is mentioned twice. You could translate the verse to read, *"... in the day you eat of it, dying,[6] you shall die.[6]"* Two ꞏeaths!

The first death was the instant spiritual separation from the life and light of God.

◗ Just imagine that moment from Adam's perspective: To have intimately known God, His glory, His thoughts, His love. Then in one horrifying moment, nothing. *Their eyes were suddenly opened*[9] to a completely different reality. Instead of being one spirit with God, they began to relate to Him from an emotional, soulish perspective. The *clothing*[4] *of glory* lifted. Naked, ashamed,

> *Then the eyes of both of them were opened,*[9] and *they knew that they were naked*; and they sewed fig leaves together and made themselves coverings. And they heard the sound of the Lord God walking in the garden in the cool of the day, and Adam and his wife hid themselves from the presence of the Lord God among the trees of the garden. Then the Lord God called to Adam and said to him, "Where are you?" So he said, "I heard Your voice in the garden, and I was *afraid*[10] because I was naked; and I hid myself." GENESIS 3:7-10

and now an ominous feeling, that was previously unknown, became a constant and formidable companion—*fear*[10] (Genesis 3:7-10).

God's perspective, His mind, His companionship, was now just a memory. The light of revelation (Introduction) had departed and Adam was filled with darkness of understanding. The cold hard manifestation of the corrupted nature must have been a stark and shocking reality.

The second death was the sudden grip of corruption at work in the flesh, the slow physical death of the body.

Being made of the same *cursed elements of the earth,*[11] Adam's body began the slow process of *dust to dust.*[13] His body came under the influence of the *curse*[11] and he began to *physically die*[13] (Genesis 3:17-19).

THE CURSED EARTH

The *earth was cursed*[11] in the same moment. Instead of all they put their hand to being blessed and fruitful, the ground would only produce *by toil and the sweat of their brow.*[12]

...*"Cursed is the ground*[11] *for your sake; in toil you shall eat of it* all the days of your life. Both thorns and thistles it shall bring forth for you. In *the sweat of your face*[12] you shall eat bread till you return to the ground, for out of it you were taken; *for dust you are, and to dust you shall return."*[13] GENESIS 3:17-19

Just like its inhabitants, *the earth groans in the bondage of corruption*[14] (Romans 8:20-23). It's subject to decay and living things die. Natural disasters are an expression of the *curse*[11] that was set in motion at the fall, not an expression of God's wrath.

For the creation was subjected to futility, not willingly, but because of Him who subjected it in hope; because *the creation itself also will be delivered from the bondage of corruption*[14] *into the glorious liberty of the children of God.*[15] For we know that *the whole creation groans* and labors with birth pangs together until now. Not only that, but we also who have the firstfruits of the Spirit, even we ourselves groan within ourselves, eagerly waiting for the adoption, the redemption of our body. ROMANS 8:20-23

Now I saw a new heaven and a *new earth,*[16] for the first heaven and the first earth had passed away... REVELATION 21:1

Along with the completion of our redemption, the earth will be *delivered into liberty*[15] as well. In Revelation 21:1, John saw in the spirit *the new earth,*[16] noting that the first earth had passed away. Undoubtedly it will surpass God's original creation.

THE NEW REALITY

Adam and Eve lost their authority and dominion over the earth. When they put their faith in the devil's word over God's Word, they simply handed over their authority as well.

> ... And now, lest he put out his hand and take also of the tree of life, and eat, and live forever"— therefore the Lord God sent him out of the garden of Eden to till the ground from which he was taken. So He drove out the man; and He placed cherubim at the east of the garden of Eden, and a flaming sword which turned every way, to guard the way to the tree of life. **GENESIS 3:22-24**

To prevent us being eternally cursed, God cast Adam and Eve out of the garden. To eat of the tree of life in this corrupted state would have sealed the curse for all of mankind with no hope of redemption. He set two cherubim at the entrance to guard the way (Genesis 3:22-24).

ABSORBING DEEPER

1/ What does the first mention of devil tell us about his tactics against us? Refer to Genesis 3:1.

_____

_____

_____

_____

_____

2/ What did Adam and Eve do that caused the fall of mankind? HINT: This is what *caused their disobedience* to God's command.

_____

_____

_____

3/ How do we do the same thing in our daily life? Give an example.

_____

_____

_____

_____

_____

4/ What are the two deaths in Genesis 2:17?

_____

_____

_____

REFLECT AND DISCUSS

5/ Observing the cursed earth, imagine two ways it must have been different according to God's original design. Does this change the way you view disasters in the natural world?

_____

_____

_____

6/ List three things Adam had before the fall that inspire you the most.

_____

_____

_____

_____

7/ 💧 Imagine the moment of *instant* spiritual separation from God that Adam experienced. Now, think about how even though Adam's body began the *slow process* of "dust-to-dust," he had no understanding of sickness and death so it took him 930 years to die.

In contrast, when we received Christ, we were given *instant* access to God's perspective and fellowship. But because we were born with no understanding of intimacy with God, it can be a *slow process* perceiving and growing in this relationship. We were born acquainted with sickness and disease, so it can be a *slow process* understanding "by His stripes we are healed" (1 Peter 2:24).

What other similarities and opposites can you see? What do you think could speed up the *slow process* of perceiving, believing and receiving?

_____

_____

_____

_____

_____

_____

_____

_____

_____

_____

8/ What effects of the curse do you see removed from your life? What effects of the curse *appear* to still be active in your life?

_____

_____

_____

_____

_____

_____

9/ Does this mean Jesus' Work isn't Finished? What's the conclusion?

_____

_____

_____

10/ Carrying on from Chapter 1, question 6, how do you need to adjust on a daily basis? HINT: How can you practically apply James 4:7 in the busyness of your life?

_____

_____

_____

_____

CHAPTER THREE

The Corrupted Nature

> Then the serpent said to the woman,
> "You will not surely die. For God knows
> that in the day you eat of it your eyes
> will be opened, and you will be like God,
> ***knowing good and evil***." GENESIS 3:4-5

The knowledge of good and evil is a state of consciousness. Adam and Eve digressed from spiritual beings that perceived God intimately, to soulish beings driven by emotions and mental reasoning. They no longer saw through God's divine perspective that knew only goodness. Their eyes were suddenly opened to knowing good and evil —an entirely different viewpoint. (Genesis 3:4-5).

❶ The first produce of the corrupted nature was that Adam and Eve, in fear and shame from condemnation, immediately hid from God's presence and tried to fix ***themselves¹*** (Genesis 3:7-10). According to the law of first mention, this is *the* most crucial understanding to observe about the fallen nature ***and ourselves.*** Even after being restored to God's

Then the eyes of both of them were opened, and they knew that they were naked; and they sewed fig leaves together and ***made themselves¹ coverings***. And they heard the sound of the Lord God walking in the garden in the cool of the day, and ***Adam and his wife hid themselves¹*** from the presence of the Lord God among the trees of the garden. Then the Lord God called to Adam and said to him, "Where are you?" So he said, "I heard Your voice in the garden, and I was afraid because I was naked; and ***I hid myself.¹***" GENESIS 3:7-10

fellowship, our tendency is to be compelled to do **works of self effort**[1] to be right with God (attempting to be more good than evil). We rely on the arm of our own flesh and leave God out of our decision-making process. This enormously overlooked perception about ourselves is a common theme throughout all of scripture. If we remain unaware of this **self-willed propensity,**[1] there is no way we'll be able to take hold of our inheritance in Christ here on earth.

❶ Having lost their spiritual covering, the shame they felt came from recognizing good and evil and being condemned by it because they were guilty— 🔒 the first picture of the law (Chapter 4). The fig leaves they sowed for coverings represent **religious works of self effort and self righteousness.**[1] Observing this first mention with this understanding, we have a good foundation for meditating on every reference to fig leaves and fig trees throughout all of scripture.

THE KNOWLEDGE OF GOOD AND EVIL

The ability to know good and evil is a curse in itself. It means that we know both good and evil, we do both, and we **judge**[2] both. In fact, we view everything through the lens of good and evil. This might seem to be a good thing on the surface, but contemplating this nature further, we can see the opposite is true.

WE KNOW GOOD AND EVIL

We can perceive and recognize good, and perceive and recognize evil.

WE DO GOOD AND EVIL

Most people want to do good, but it's impossible to *only* do good. The nature that knows good and evil is compelled to do *both* good *and* evil.

WE JUDGE GOOD AND EVIL

This nature comes with a set of scales. **Automatically and unconsciously,** we tend to **judge**[2] our good works more highly and downplay our evil works. By this method we feel better and justify ourselves as "good" people—we have a weightier "good" balance to our scales.

Automatically and unconsciously, we *esire* to ***judge*** [2] others and we do so with a different bias. Recognizing another person's evil gives us the illusion of being more righteous and safer from God's judgment.

> Therefore you are inexcusable, O man, whoever you are who ***judge,*** [2] for in whatever you judge another you condemn yourself; for you who ***judge*** [2] practice the same things. ROMANS 2:1
>
> There is a way that seems right to a man, but its end is the way of death. **PROVERBS 14:12**

But here is the hypocritical dilemma. We simply have no correct standing to ***judge*** [2] ***ourselves or others*** since we are guilty accusers (Romans 2:1).

Most people would weigh or ***judge*** [2] themselves as not perfect but mostly good. But this way of ***self judgment,*** [2] that seems right to a man, literally leads to death (Proverbs 14:12). Only God can correctly ***judge*** [2] and his scale of judgment is completely different than ours.

BORN INTO THE CORRUPTED NATURE

It's important to note that doing evil, or sins, isn't what makes a person a sinner. Rather, ***sins are a natural outworking, or the fruit of the corrupted sin nature.*** [3] Without being washed by the blood of Christ and indwelt by the Holy Spirit, sin has dominion over all of unregenerate mankind. It dominates us and we have no ability to ***permanently*** control the lust of the flesh or the evil desire of the heart. Even amongst "good" works, we are slaves to sin (Ephesians 2:1-3).

> And you He made alive, who were dead in trespasses and sins, in which you once walked according to the course of this world, according to the prince of the power of the air, the spirit who now works in the sons of disobedience, among whom also ***we all once conducted ourselves*** in the lusts of our flesh, fulfilling the desires of the flesh and of the mind, and were ***by nature children of wrath,*** [3] just as the others. **EPHESIANS 2:1-3**

But it was ***through one man that sin entered the world—Adam.***[4] We didn't do the sin of Adam, yet we were all born into the corruption *that he cause*• (Romans 5:12). Without the Holy Spirit, we are compelled to act according to our ***sin nature***[3]*—an• Go• knows it.*

> Therefore, just as ***through one man sin entered the world,***[4] and death through sin, and thus death spread to all men, because all sinned— **ROMANS 5:12**

 In fact, God knew it from the very beginning and designed the way back to perfect relationship with Him.

> ..that God was in Christ ***reconciling the world to Himself,***[5] not imputing their trespasses to them... **2 CORINTHIANS 5:19**
>
> For it pleased the Father that in Him all the fullness should dwell, and ***by Him to reconcile all things to Himself,***[5] by Him, whether things on earth or things in heaven, having made peace through the blood of His cross. **COLOSSIANS 1:19-20**
>
> For by grace you have been saved through faith, and that not of yourselves; it is the gift of God, not of works, lest anyone should boast. **EPHESIANS 2:8-9**

It is God who is ***reconciling all of us to Himself***[5] through the Finished Work of Christ, not imputing our trespasses against us (2 Corinthians 5:19, Colossians 1:19-20). It is essential this free gift of redemption is *receive*• by each and every one of us (Ephesians 2:8-9, Chapter 13).

So having been born into the corrupted ***sin nature,***[3] God had to show us something that we could not possibly see or understand by ourselves. He introduced the law to open our eyes.

ABSORBING DEEPER

1/ What did the corrupt nature first produce?

_____

2/ What is the judgment and condemnation that comes from knowing good and evil a picture of?

_____

3/ Why isn't the knowledge of good and evil a good thing?

_____

_____

_____

4/ What have we all been born into? Who caused it?

_____

_____

5/ What did God do about it?

_____

_____

6/ What came first; sin or the sin nature? What should we expect from the sin nature?

_____

_____

_____

7/ What did God do to open our eyes?

_____

_____

REFLECT AND DISCUSS

8/ Can you recognize ways you have automatically and unconsciously operated from good and evil thinking? What are some examples where you have judged others and yourself?

_____
_____
_____
_____
_____
_____

9/ How does this help us understand our own tendencies even after we have received Christ?

_____
_____
_____
_____
_____
_____

10/ Can you explain the difference between doing sins and having a corrupted sin nature?

_____
_____
_____
_____
_____
_____

CHAPTER FOUR

The Purpose of the Law

> Therefore by the deeds of the law no flesh will be justified in His sight, for **by the law is the knowledge of sin.** ROMANS 3:20

The law written on tablets of stone was never meant to justify us, perfect us and bring us back into fellowship with God the Father (Romans 3:20). Having been born into corruption, mankind had no reference point to understand that we were not living God's intended plan. How could we? Only Adam understood the original creation and relationship with God the Father. So the whole purpose of the law was to open our eyes and show us several things:

1. To understand what sin and the sin nature is, and what its wages are—a sentence of condemnation unto death and eternal separation from God (Ephesians 2:3, Romans 6:23).

2. To show us the righteous requirement of the law —perfection or death. There are no scales of good that can outweigh the evil (James 2:10).

> among whom also we all once conducted ourselves in the lusts of our flesh, fulfilling the desires of the flesh and of the mind, and **were by nature children of wrath,** just as the others. EPHESIANS 2:3
>
> The wages of sin is death... ROMANS 6:23
>
> For whoever shall keep the whole law, and yet stumble in one point, he is guilty of all. JAMES 2:10

3. To show us that we are cursed by the law—we can't escape this sentence of death (Galatians 3:10).

4. To show us that it is impossible to keep the law in our own strength. Attempting to be justified by it causes us to fall from grace and we make Christ of no effect (Galatians 5:2-4, Galatians 2:21 KJV).

> ..."Cursed is everyone who does not continue in all things which are written in the book of the law, to do them." **GALATIANS 3:10**
>
> Behold, I Paul say unto you, that if ye be circumcised, ***Christ shall profit you nothing***. For I testify again to every man that is circumcised, that he is a debtor to do the whole law. ***Christ is become of no effect unto you, whosoever of you are justified by the law;*** ye are fallen from grace. **GALATIANS 5:2-4 KJV**
>
> I do not frustrate the grace of God: for if righteousness come by the law, then Christ is dead in vain. **GALATIANS 2:21 KJV**

THE SELF RIGHTEOUS NATURE

In Exodus 24:7, Moses read the Book of the Covenant to the leaders of the tribe of Israel. Their first response demonstrates perfectly the *self righteous propensity*[1] of the sin nature and the good and evil consciousness—the typical desire *to be and do good*[1] and the inability to truly do it. They said, *"... we will do it and be obedient."*[1] Yet just a few chapters later, they molded a false god from gold, worshiped it and fell into all manner of sinful behavior (Exodus 32:8).

There is nothing that God is more heartbroken about than *self righteousness.*[1] Throughout all of scripture, God's wrath is pointed more towards *self works,*[1] and *self justification*[1] than sinful behavior itself.

> Then he took the Book of the Covenant and read in the hearing of the people. And they said, "All that the LORD has said ***we will do, and be obedient."***[1] **EXODUS 24:7**
>
> They have turned aside quickly out of the way which I commanded them. They have made themselves a molded calf, and worshiped it and sacrificed to it, and said, This is your god, O Israel, that brought you out of the land of Egypt!' " **EXODUS 32:8**

God knows the sin nature causes us to sin just as surely as a duck quacks because it is a duck. But God mourns over **self righteousness**[1] above all **because it prevents us from seeing our need for our Savior** and eagerly receiving His plan of redemption through Christ; His amazing free gift of grace.

> Moreover **the law entered that the offense might abound.**[2] But where sin abounded, **grace abounded much more,**[3] so that as sin reigned in death, even so grace might reign through righteousness to eternal life through Jesus Christ our Lord **ROMANS 5:20-21**

So while the corrupted sin nature yearns to **justify itself,**[1] the law is the perfect instrument to show us the futility. It captures us by our desire to **do works to justify ourselves,**[1] while simultaneously showing us the impossibility (Romans 5:20-21).

In fact, **the law even gives power to sin and causes it to abound.**[2] If you've ever caught yourself saying, "I'll never do *that* again," you can bet *"that"* is exactly what you will do. You have essentially put yourself under the law, and condemned yourself by your own words.

KEY GREEK WORD

5248 HUPERPERISSEUÓ:[3] (hoop-er-per-is-syoo'-o) to abound more exceedingly. † From **5228 HYPÉR**, beyond and **4052 PERISSEÚŌ**, abundantly, exceeding. Beyond what already exceeds. Ultra (super) abounds.

But Romans 5:20-21 very clearly states the purpose of the law—that the grace brought through Jesus Christ **exceedingly abounds much more,**[3] and righteousness through Him to eternal life!

CHOOSING GOD'S REMEDY

> that God was in Christ reconciling the world to Himself, not imputing their trespasses to them...
> **2 CORINTHIANS 5:19**

The law opens our eyes to clearly see the corruption we desperately need to be saved from, and it is God who designed this pathway back to fellowship with Him (2 Corinthians 5:19).

While it was one man's **disobedience**[4] that caused us all to be born into the corrupted sin nature, so much greater is the one Man, Jesus, who was **perfectly obedient**[5] to go all the way to the Cross (Romans 5:19 and Chapter 5). Through this act, He paid the price of the wages of *our* sin **once and for all** (Romans 6:23).

God is the one reconciling the world *to Himself* through the Finished Work, but the choice to receive His gift of grace is ours. The only requirement to receive is to say "yes" by believing with out heart and confessing with our mouth (Romans 10:9-10, Chapter 13).

> For as by one man's **disobedience**[4] many were made sinners, so also by one Man's **obedience**[5] many will be made righteous ROMANS 5:19
>
> that if you confess with your mouth the Lord Jesus and believe in your heart that God has raised Him from the dead, you will be saved. For **with the heart one believes unto righteousness, and with the mouth confession is made unto salvation.** ROMANS 10:9-10

FROM OLD COVENANT TO THE NEW

The Old Covenant is characterized by the law written on tablets of stone, and the ordinances of the temple perpetually ministered by the high priests. It has been **made obsolete** by the New and will soon pass away entirely (Hebrews 8:13).

This doesn't contradict Matthew 5:17-18. Jesus didn't do away with the law, **He fulfilled it** by completing our sentence for us.

For the unsaved world, the law still applies. It's essential for continuing its original purpose —to convict the world of sin by revealing the sin nature and separation from God.

> In that He says, "A new covenant," **He has made the first obsolete.** Now what is becoming obsolete and growing old is ready to vanish away. HEBREWS 8:13
>
> "Do not think that I have come to abolish the Law or the Prophets; **I have not come to abolish them but to fulfill them.** For assuredly, I say to you, till heaven and earth pass away, one jot or one tittle will by no means pass from the law till all is fulfilled. MATTHEW 5:17-18

This is His way of pointing us to Jesus. One day there will be no opportunity left to accept His free gift through Christ—the age of grace is drawing to a close (Chapter 12). Today is the day of salvation (Chapter 13)!

THE COURT OF HEAVEN SATISFIED

God can't simply overlook sin. If He did, He would be unjust. The very act of allowing some sin would taint Him with it.

The sentence of our condemnation had to be completed. Only through a blood sacrifice could the law be fully satisfied. Only a perfect substitute, a spotless lamb (Chapter 10, Part 3C) could take our place and wash away the sin of all mankind eternally.

Jesus, the Son of God, is the only perfect lamb. His sacrifice was the only way that we could be restored to right standing with God the Father. So *He became a curse for us* and redeemed us from the

> Christ has redeemed us from the curse of the law, *having become a curse for us* (for it is written, "Cursed is everyone who hangs on a tree"), that the blessing of Abraham might come upon the Gentiles in Christ Jesus, that we might receive the promise of the Spirit through faith. **GALATIANS 3:13-14**

curse of the law (Galatians 3:13-14). Judicially, God can now *justify us eternally by His blood,* which is the proof and evidence that the sentence of our condemnation has been fully paid. By it, the law has been fulfilled for all who receive Him (Chapter 13).

ABSORBING DEEPER

1/ What was the law never meant to do?

_____

2/ In your own words, summarize what the law is supposed to do instead. HINT: God knows the sin nature, by its nature, does sin.

_____

_____

_____

3/ Why is self-righteousness worse than sin itself? Do you know people who "don't need God?"

_____

_____

_____

4/ What does the sin nature yearn to do?

_____

5/ What does "the law entered so that sin might abound" mean (Romans 5:20-21)? What abounds more than sin?

_____

_____

_____

6/ What is God's remedy for Romans 5:12 (page 21) and how does Romans 5:19 define it?

_____

_____

_____

7/ How has the law been made obsolete?

_____

_____

8/ How has the court of heaven been fully satisfied?

_____

_____

REFLECT AND DISCUSS

9/ Self-righteousness, self-effort and self-works are the result of being separated from God. The unredeemed mind thinks independence from God is a good thing. Can you see why the opposite is true? What negative effects can you (still) see in your own life?

_____

_____

_____

_____

_____

10/With the clarity of understanding the self-righteous nature and the purpose of the law, how do you view your unsaved friends and family differently? How might your conversation change? HINT: Judgment pushes people away. The love of God draws people to repentance.

_____

_____

_____

_____

_____

11/Do you understand why God had to bring in the law to open our eyes? Think about what we couldn't possibly know if it wasn't for the law.

_____

_____

_____

_____

_____

12/How does this chapter change the way you have understood God's design of salvation through the Finished Work of Christ?

_____

_____

_____

_____

_____

13/How has the true purpose of the law changed your understanding of the Christian life? How will this change how you conduct your life?

_____

_____

_____

_____

_____

CHAPTER FIVE

The Abrahamic Covenant

> Now the Lord had said to Abram: "Get out of your country, from your family and from your father's house, to a land that I will show you. ***I will make you a great nation;*** I will bless you and make your name great; and you shall be a blessing. I will bless those who bless you, and I will curse him who curses you; ***and in you all the families of the earth shall be blessed."***[1]
> **GENESIS 12:1-3**

There is another covenant that applies to us in Christ.  Through believing in Jesus and the Finished Work, we take part in the Abrahamic Covenant.

Way before the law was given to Moses, we are introduced to Abram, and his wife Sarai, who was barren. God told Abram to leave his father's house to go to the land he would show him and He promised He would make him a great nation—***all the families of the earth would be blessed through him***[1] (Genesis 12:1-3).

About ten years later, Sarai was well beyond child-bearing. But God reassured Abram of His promise to make him a great nation ***through***

> Then Abram said, "Look, You have given me no offspring; indeed one born in my house is my heir!" And behold, the word of the Lord came to him, saying, "This one shall not be your heir, but one **who will come from your own body** shall be your heir." Then He brought him outside and said, ***"Look now toward heaven, and count the stars*** if you are able to number them." And He said to him, "So shall your descendants be." And **he believed[2] in the Lord,** and **He accounted it to him[3] for righteousness.[4]** GENESIS 15:3-6

his own seed. He gave him a powerful ***visual picture of the stars*** to keep his eyes fixed in faith (Genesis 15:3-6).

Abram believed[2] God's word, not circumstances. Even though he faltered, he didn't give in to the voice of the devil tempting him to doubt God (Chapters 1 and 2). Instead, Abram was fixed on God's promise and ***it was accounted to him[3] for righteousness.[4]*** This means ***righteousness,[4]*** with all its rights and privileges, was ***reckoned to Abram's account[3] by faith.[2]***

> When Abram was ninety-nine years old, the Lord appeared to Abram and said to him, "I am Almighty God; walk before Me and be blameless. And **I will make My covenant between Me and you,[5]** and will multiply you exceedingly." Then Abram fell on his face, and God talked with him, saying: "As for Me, behold, My covenant is with you, and you shall be a father of many nations. **No longer shall your name be called Abram, but your name shall be Abraham; for I have made you a father of many nations.** I will make you exceedingly fruitful; and I will make nations of you, and kings shall come from you. And **I will establish My covenant[5] between Me and you and your descendants after you in their generations, for an everlasting covenant,[5] to be God to you and your descendants after you.** GENESIS 17:1-7

Finally in Genesis 17:1-7, God **bound Himself in an eternal covenant[5] with Abram** and changed his name to **Abraham**, "father of nations."

Taking an extremely brief look into Hebrew alphabet and number meanings, God added the hey, representing the breath of God, to Abram's name and he became Abra**ha**m. The fifth letter of the Hebrew alphabet, hey, is the number of grace. 🌢 God essentially breathed His breath, His life, His grace into Abraham and through it, He established the ***covenant[5] promise of righteousness[4] by faith.[2]***

What was it that Abraham believed? The same gospel of grace that is preached to us, Abraham believed on the Messiah (Galatians 3:8).

> And the Scripture, foreseeing that God would justify the Gentiles by faith, **preached the gospel to Abraham** beforehand, saying, **"In you all the nations shall be blessed."**[1] GALATIANS 3:8
>
> **For God so loved the world that He gave His only begotten Son,** that whoever believes in Him should not perish but have everlasting life. JOHN 3:16
>
> Then God said to Abraham, "As for Sarai your wife, you shall not call her name Sarai, but Sarah shall be her name. **And I will bless her and also give you a son by her;** then I will bless her, and she shall be **a mother of nations;** kings of peoples shall be from her." GENESIS 17:15-16

So when God gave us His only son, Jesus (John 3:16), this was the fulfillment of the gospel preached to Abraham and the gift of grace.

Sarai received the same breath of God and became Sar**ah**, **a mother of nations.** (Genesis 17:15-16). A year later, at the ripe old age of 99, she gave birth to a son, the heir of the promise.

A LEGALLY BINDING AGREEMENT

In a covenant agreement, the greater party binds themselves in a pledge to perform something to benefit and cover the lesser party. It doesn't end at the death of the lesser party, but passes to their heirs. Since God never dies, any **covenant**[5] made by Him is **eternal and irrevocable** (Hebrews 13:20).

> Now may the God of peace who brought up our Lord Jesus from the dead, that great Shepherd of the sheep, through the blood of the **everlasting covenant,**[5] HEBREWS 13:20
>
> And if you are Christ's, then you are Abraham's seed, and **heirs according to the promise.** GALATIANS 3:29

🦶 According to Galatians 3:29, all of us who believe in Jesus' Finished Work are smack-dab in the middle of this **covenant**[5] and **heirs according to the promise!**[1] We are **all the families of earth that are eternally blessed!**[1] Abraham is our father of faith—we have the same faith in Christ as he did and **our faith**[2] **is accounted to us**[3] **as righteousness.**[4]

> For he hath made him to be sin for us, who knew no sin; *that we might be made the righteousness of God in him.*[4] 2 CORINTHIANS 5:21 KJV
>
> For I am not ashamed of the gospel of Christ, for *it is the power of God to salvation for everyone who believes,* for the Jew first and also for the Greek. For in it *the righteousness of God*[4] *is revealed* from faith to faith; as it is written, *"The just*[6] *shall live by faith."*[2] ROMANS 1:16-17

We've moved from faith in the picture of the Old Covenant, to faith in the substance—Jesus (Chapter 4). We who believe <u>*have been made* the righteousness of God in Christ</u>[4] (2 Corinthians 5:21). We are the <u>*justified*</u>[6] *who live by faith*[2] and this is *the faith we live by*—we believe the Finished Work of Christ and every promise and reassurance of God that now applies to us (Romans 1:16-17).

THE BLESSINGS OF THE RIGHTEOUS

Now we can rightfully claim for ourselves every scripture that declares the privileges of a righteous man, the blameless, or the upright. Not because of our righteousness, but because of the gift of *Jesus' righteousness*[4] given to us (Romans 5:17). Not because of our perfect obedience, but *Jesus' perfect obedience*[7] to fully carry out our sentence of condemnation (Romans 5:19). Like Abraham, we qualify to receive every blessing because we have been made the *righteousness of God in Christ*[4] *by faith*[2] in Jesus' Finished Work. <u>This truly is why the gospel is such good news!</u>

> For if by the one man's offense death reigned through the one, much more those who receive abundance of grace and of *the gift of righteousness*[4] will reign in life through the One, Jesus Christ.) ROMANS 5:17
>
> For as by one man's disobedience many were made sinners, so also by one Man's *obedience*[7] many *will be made righteous*[4] ROMANS 5:19

Let's look at a few examples of declarations of God's protection and favor upon the righteous which must be received *by faith*[2] *in Christ and His obedience*[7] (Proverbs 11:8, 12:21, 10:3). If we walk through the *troubles*[8] of life looking to be

> The righteous is delivered from *trouble,*[8] but the wicked takes his place. PROVERBS 11:8 NASB

delivered based on our own righteousness we'll be subject to the condemnation of the enemy and our faith will fail every time. (Chapter 6). Full of fear and unbelief, unconsciously we'll be prompted to do self works to right wrongs in an attempt to qualify ourselves (Chapter 7). The devil's desire is that we remain unaware of this thinking where we have *fallen from grace*[9] and are subject to the curse in the earth (Galatians 5:4, Chapters 1 and 2).

But none of these promises, nor dozens of others, can be claimed based on self works (Chapter 4). None of us are blameless, upright or righteous of ourselves, *not one* (Romans 3:10). No one on the face of the planet would have ever been able to claim any of them.

So that none can boast of ourselves, believing in Jesus and *His perfect obedience*[7] to carry out the Finished Work is the only way we qualify to receive the precious *gift of His righteousness*[4] (Ephesians 2:8-9). Being in *right standing*[4] with God, not only do we have eternal life, but all the benefits and privileges of the righteous, the blameless and the upright, His *righteousness*[4] being fully *reckoned to our account.*[3]

> No harm befalls the righteous, but the wicked are filled with *trouble.*[8] PROVERBS 12:21 NASB
>
> The Lord will not allow the righteous to hunger, but He will reject the craving of the wicked. PROVERBS 10:3 NASB
>
> You have become estranged from Christ, you who attempt to be justified by law; you have *fallen from grace.*[9] GALATIANS 5:4
>
> ... "There is none righteous, no, not one; ROMANS 3:10
>
> For by grace you have been saved through faith, and that not of yourselves; *it is the gift of God,* not of works, lest anyone should boast. EPHESIANS 2:8-9

This is God's true *righteousness*[4] *revealed* and brought to the light of our understanding (Romans 1:16-17 p35). We can unashamedly take hold of every blessing of the righteous *by faith.*[2] We can go boldly to the Throne of *grace,*[9] having obtained mercy through the blood of Christ, and find *grace*[9] *to help* for every need—His supernatural provision (Hebrews 4:16).

> Let us therefore come boldly to the throne of grace, that we may obtain mercy and find *grace*[9] *to help* in time of need. HEBREWS 4:16

TEARING DOWN THE ARGUMENTS OF THE ENEMY

> ...For the weapons of our warfare are not carnal but mighty in God for pulling down strongholds, **casting down arguments** and every high thing that exalts itself against the knowledge of God, bringing every thought into captivity **to the obedience of Christ,**[7]
> **2 CORINTHIANS 10:4-5**

Through this correct understanding and application of **Christ's perfect obedience,**[7] every cunning argument of the devil is completely demolished (2 Corinthians 10:4-5). We'll stop falling for his endless attempts to get us on cursed, "self-effort" ground. We'll recognize and take captive every thought before the lies of lack and fear overrun our heart and become the confession of our mouth. We'll be able to consciously hold every argument next to **Christ's perfect obedience,**[7] recognize and apply the corresponding provision that is ours because of the Finished Work, and thoroughly cast down every deception.

When we are secure that our standing of **righteousness**[4] has nothing to do with us and everything to do with Him, we can't be tossed to and fro in unbelief. The **faith**[2] required to access His **grace**[9] will automatically undergird our every

> For You, O Lord, will bless the **righteous;**[4] with favor You will surround him as with a shield. **PSALM 5:12**
>
> ... The effective, fervent prayer of a **righteous**[4] man avails much. **JAMES 5:16**

word and action, no matter how the circumstances of life appear. We know we are surrounded with favor and our prayers from **faith**[2] affect powerful change (Psalm 5:12, James 5:16). Resting in **faith**[2] until we see His supernatural provision (as opposed to our natural provision) will become our instinctive and normal expectation. This describes the normal supernatural life of the mature believer. Through maintaining this focus, the devil's arguments don't hold any power over us anymore.

DEUTERONOMY 28 BLESSINGS AND CURSES

Looking at this incredible list of the Lord's protection, favor, provision and health upon the **diligently obedient,** we could be quick to disqualify ourselves. But by **faith**[2] in Christ, **His perfect obedience**[7] qualifies us to

> "Now it shall come to pass, **if you diligently obey** the voice of the Lord your God, to observe carefully all His commandments which I command you today, that the Lord your God will set you high above all nations of the earth. And **all these blessings shall come upon you and overtake you,** because you obey the voice of the Lord your God: "Blessed shall you be in the city, and blessed shall you be in the country. "Blessed shall be the fruit of your body, the produce of your ground... **DEUTERONOMY 28:1-4**

> "But it shall come to pass, **if you do not obey** the voice of the Lord your God, to observe carefully all His commandments and His statutes which I command you today, that **all these curses will come upon you and overtake you:** "Cursed shall you be in the city, and cursed shall you be in the country. "Cursed shall be your basket and your kneading bowl. "Cursed shall be the fruit of your body and the produce of your land... **DEUTERONOMY 28:15-18**

receive it all. By *faith*[2] these blessings come upon us, even overtake us (Deuteronomy 28:1-4, look up the whole list through v14).

Conversely the much longer list of curses upon the disobedient will fill us with dread if we don't understand our *gift of righteousness in Christ*[4] (Deuteronomy 28:15-18, look up the whole list through v68).

THE BLESSING OF ABRAHAM

Christ redeemed us from the curse of the law *so that* we could receive *the blessing of Abraham* (Galatians 3:13-14). Completely different from blessings of provision and favor, the blessing of Abraham is *justification*[6] *by faith.*[2] We receive it as a gift through faith in the Finished Work of Christ, not of ourselves. (Ephesians 2:8-9 p36).

Having been *freely justified*[6] *eternally,* there is nothing that can change our *right standing*[4] with God (Romans 3:24).

> Christ has redeemed us from the curse of the law, having become a curse for us (for it is written, "Cursed is everyone who hangs on a tree"), *that the blessing of Abraham* might come upon the Gentiles in Christ Jesus, *that* we might receive the promise of the Spirit through faith. **GALATIANS 3:13–14**

> being *justified*[6] *freely* by His grace through the redemption that is in Christ Jesus, **ROMANS 3:24**

Blessed be the God and Father of our Lord Jesus Christ, ***who has blessed us with every spiritual blessing in the heavenly places in Christ,*** just as He chose us in Him before the foundation of the world, that we should be ***holy and without blame***[6] before Him in love, having predestined us to adoption as sons by Jesus Christ to Himself, according to the good pleasure of His will, to the praise of the glory of His grace, by which ***He made us accepted in the Beloved.***[6] EPHESIANS 1:3-6

What then shall we say to these things? ***If God is for us, who can be against us?*** He who did not spare His own Son, but delivered Him up for us all, ***how shall He not with Him also freely give us all things?***[1] Who shall bring a charge against God's elect? It is God who ***justifies.***[6] ROMANS 8:31-33

No failure of ourselves, no lie of the devil, our forgiveness is eternal.

We have been made ***acceptable to God***[6] by the Finished Work. He's the one who has ***eternally justified***[6] us (Ephesians 1:3-6). What can possibly come against us? We righteously qualify in Christ for every provision of ***His grace,***[9] and He freely and ***justly***[6] ***gives us all things***[1] (Romans 8:31-33).

GOD'S COVENANT LOYALTY TOWARD US

God is not a man that should lie (Numbers 23:19). If He said it, we can take it to the bank and make a withdrawal! He gave His Word to us by his own name and ***magnified His Word above His name***. Meditating on this we will receive ***boldness and strength***[11] in our thought life as we rest in Him and His unbreakable promises (Psalm 138:2-3).

"God is not a man, that He should lie, nor a son of man, that He should repent. Has He said, and will He not do? Or has He spoken, and will He not make it good? NUMBERS 23:19

I will worship toward Your holy temple, And praise Your name For Your ***lovingkindness***[10] and Your truth; For ***You have magnified Your word above all Your name.*** In the day when I cried out, You answered me, And made me ***bold with strength***[11] in my soul. PSALM 138:2–3

KEY HEBREW WORD

2617 CHECED:[10] (kheh'-sed) *favor,* goodness, kindness. § In keeping the covenants, with Abraham, with Moses and Israel.

KEY GREEK WORD

1656 ELEOS:[10] *mercy,* pity, compassion. Translating 2617 checed (covenant-loyalty, covenant-love in the OT over 170 times) *Mercy as it is defined by loyalty to God's covenant.*

The word *lovingkindness*[10] found here and repeated throughout scripture could be translated as *covenant loyalty.*[10] Accordingly, we can understand that God's *love and kindness* He lavished upon us through the Finished Work

> Surely goodness and *lovingkindness*[10] will follow me all the days of my life, and I will dwell in the house of the Lord forever. **PSALM 23:6 NASB**

is backed by His *covenant loyalty*[10] that arises from the Abrahamic Covenant. His *lovingkindness*[10] *is* His *mercy and grace.* The God of heaven and earth has literally bound Himself to us to *bless us*[1] beyond all we can even imagine. It's this *covenant loyalty*[10] that follows us all the days of our life (Psalm 23:6)!

The power of God is in His gospel of Him having *freely justified*[6] us and *freely given us all things*[1] (Romans 1:16-17 p35). We have a right to claim "all things." It's part of our inheritance, not by a self-righteous claim but a *righteous claim in Christ.*[4]

> But *without faith*[2] *it is impossible to please Him,*[12] for he who comes to God must believe that He is, and that He is a rewarder of those who *diligently seek Him.*[13] **HEBREWS 11:6**

It is one of God's greatest delights[12] to see us learn to put a *faith*[2] *demand* on everything that is ours in Christ. When we believe God, the devil's voice that continually tries to get us to doubt Him (Chapter 2) is silenced. As we *diligently seek*[13] to continually grow in our understanding of this amazing *covenant*[5] relationship, we will find Him! (Hebrews 11:6)

ABSORBING DEEPER

1/ How do we take part in the Abrahamic Covenant?

_____

2/ What was reckoned to Abraham's account and how?

_____ was reckoned to Abraham's account by _____ .

3/ What did Abraham believe? HINT: Galatians 3:8.

_____

4/ In your own words, describe how we are heirs of this covenant and what it entitles us to?

_____

_____

_____

_____

_____

_____

5/ How long does this covenant last?_____

_____

6/ According to 2 Corinthians 5:21, what have we been made?

_____

_____

7/ How do we qualify?_____

_____

_____

8/ According to Galatians 3:13-14, Christ redeemed us from the

_____ so that the

_____ might come upon us,

so that we could receive _____

through faith.

9/ What is the blessing of Abraham?_____

_____

10/How have we been made right in God's eyes and for how long?
Could God change His mind or break the covenant? Why or why not?
HINT: What is the accurate translation of the word lovingkindness?

_____

_____

_____

11/Could *we* break the covenant or disqualify ourselves in any way?
Why or why not? _____

_____

_____

REFLECT AND DISCUSS

12/Understanding the benefits and privileges of being the righteousness
of God in Christ is truly how we understand the Good News of the
Gospel. Write down some benefits you didn't realize were yours.

_____

_____

_____

_____

_____

13/Are you totally convinced you qualify to claim them all? What thinking could make you unsure? How does the devil try to deceive us?

_____

_____

_____

_____

_____

14/How can we go boldly and unashamedly to the Throne of grace?

_____

_____

_____

_____

_____

15/Take some time to think about how Romans 8:31-33 applies to you in your day-to-day life.

_____

_____

_____

_____

_____

16/What would it mean to live out Romans 1:16-17 (p35)?

_____

_____

_____

_____

_____

CHAPTER SIX

A Picture of Righteousness Through Romans

The book of Romans is considered to be the "Magna Carta" of New Testament doctrine. It establishes the principles of *justification by faith* which results in *true righteousness and godliness by grace.*

Taking a birds eye (biblical survey) view through chapters one through twelve, we will get a summary glimpse of the whole and gain an accurate perspective of our position in Christ because of the Finished Work. Correctly understanding this epistle, we will not only be able to navigate the whole Bible, but our Christian walk will be solidly built upon the foundations of *eternal justification, righteousness by faith* and *access to grace by faith.*

ROMANS 1

SUMMARY UNDERSTANDING: Sinners aren't righteous. No one has an excuse because everyone has a knowing inside about sin and unrighteousness.

> For the wrath of God is revealed from heaven against all ungodliness and unrighteousness of men, who suppress the truth in unrighteousness, because what may be known of God is manifest in them, *for God has shown it to them.* ROMANS 1:18-19

ROMANS 2

SUMMARY UNDERSTANDING: The religious people trying to keep the law aren't righteous. It is impossible to keep the law perfectly.

> For circumcision is indeed profitable if you keep the law; but if you are a breaker of the law, your circumcision has become uncircumcision. **ROMANS 2:25**

ROMANS 3

SUMMARY UNDERSTANDING: None are righteous. Everyone has sinned and the law makes us guilty. No one is justified by the works of the law.

> As it is written: "There is none righteous, no, not one; **ROMANS 3:10**
>
> for all have sinned and fall short of the glory of God, **ROMANS 3:23**
>
> Now we know that whatever the law says, it says to those who are under the law, that every mouth may be stopped, and all the world may become guilty before God. Therefore **by the deeds of the law no flesh will be justified in His sight**, for by the law is the knowledge of sin. **ROMANS 3:19-20**

ROMANS 4

SUMMARY UNDERSTANDING: Righteousness is reckoned through believing God. In the opposite way, working for righteousness results in a debt to keep the whole law.

> For if Abraham was justified by works, he has something to boast about, but not before God. For what does the Scripture say? "Abraham believed God, and it was accounted to him for righteousness." **Now to him who works, the wages are not counted as grace but as debt.** But to him who does not work but believes on Him who justifies the ungodly, his faith is accounted for righteousness, **ROMANS 4:2-5**

ROMANS 5

SUMMARY UNDERSTANDING: In the same way we didn't do the sin of Adam that caused our sin nature, we can't do righteous acts to be made righteous. Only Jesus perfect righteous act results in the free gift of righteousness to all who believe. The **law⁴** makes sin abound, but **grace² exceedingly overabounds¹** through Jesus. Grace is always greater than sin.

> Therefore, **just as through one man sin entered the world,** and death through sin, and thus death spread to all men, because all sinned— **ROMANS 5:12**
>
> Nevertheless death reigned from Adam to Moses, **even over those who had not sinned according to the likeness of the transgression of Adam,** who is a type of Him who was to come. **ROMANS 5:14**
>
> Therefore, as through one man's offense judgment came to all men, resulting in condemnation, even so through one Man's righteous act the free gift came to all men, resulting in justification of life. **For as by one man's disobedience many were made sinners, so also by one Man's obedience many will be made righteous.** Moreover **the law entered that the offense might abound**. But where sin abounded, **grace abounded much more,¹** so that as sin reigned in death, even so grace might reign through righteousness to eternal life through Jesus Christ our Lord. **ROMANS 5:18-21**

ROMANS 6

SUMMARY UNDERSTANDING: Jesus paid the penalty of sin for all mankind, so the **law⁴** doesn't apply to us in Christ. Under **grace,²** we reckon ourselves dead to sin and it has no dominion over us anymore.

> For the death that He died, **He died to sin once for all;** but the life that He lives, He lives to God. Likewise you also, **reckon yourselves to be dead indeed to sin**, but alive to God in Christ Jesus our Lord. **ROMANS 6:10-11**
>
> For **sin shall not have dominion over you, for you are not under law but under grace.²** **ROMANS 6:14**
>
> And having been set free from sin, you became slaves of righteousness. **ROMANS 6:18**

ROMANS 7

SUMMARY UNDERSTANDING: Being under the law in the Old Covenant is likened to being bound in marriage. When the husband dies, the woman is freed from the covenant of marriage. In the same way, sin and the law have died. *We have been freed from the Old Covenant and married to Christ and grace in the New Covenant.[3]*

Sin was aroused by the law,[4] but now apart from the law, sin is dead. *Even though sin exists in the flesh,[7] through Christ, it has no dominion over us.[8]*

We will not sin as we walk *by the leading of the Spirit,[5]* rather than by trying to keep *the letter of the law.[6]*

> Therefore, my brethren, *you also have become dead to the law through the body of Christ, that you may be married to another[3]* —to Him who was raised from the dead, that we should bear fruit to God. For when we were in the flesh, the *sinful passions which were aroused by the law[4]* were at work in our members to bear fruit to death. But now we have been delivered from the law, having died to what we were held by, *so that we should serve in the newness of the Spirit[5] and not in the oldness of the letter.[6]* ROMANS 7:4-6
>
> But sin, taking opportunity by the commandment, produced in me all manner of evil desire. For apart from the law sin was dead. ROMANS 7:8
>
> I find then a law, that evil is present with me, the one who wills to do good. For I delight in the law of God according to the inward man. *But I see another law in my members, warring against the law of my mind, and bringing me into captivity to the law of sin which is in my members.[7]* O wretched man that I am! *Who will deliver me from this body of death? I thank God—through Jesus Christ our Lord![8]* So then, with the mind I myself serve the law of God, but with the flesh the law of sin. ROMANS 7:21-25

ROMANS 8

SUMMARY UNDERSTANDING: ***There is therefore now no condemnation to us***[7] as we live the Spirit-empowered life. We are not controlled by the sin nature, but even if we succumb to the flesh, God gave Jesus who ***condemned sin in the flesh,***[13] ***and fulfilled the righteous requirement of the law in us.***[14]

Walking according to the flesh[8] is attempting to keep the law through self effort. Living under ***the law of sin and death***[11] accentuates the ***weakness of the flesh.***[12]

Walking according to the Spirit,[9] led by the New Creation heart, we are under the ***law of the Spirit of life in Christ Jesus***[10] and empowered by the Holy Spirit to godly behavior and righteous living.

There is therefore now no condemnation[7] to those who are in Christ Jesus, who do not ***walk according to the flesh,***[8] but ***according to the Spirit.***[9] For ***the law of the Spirit of life in Christ Jesus***[10] has made me free from ***the law of sin and death.***[11] For what the law could not do in that it was ***weak through the flesh,***[12] God did by sending His own Son in the likeness of sinful flesh, on account of sin: ***He condemned sin in the flesh,***[13] that ***the righteous requirement of the law might be fulfilled in us***[14] who do not walk according to the flesh but according to the Spirit. **ROMANS 8:1-4**

What shall we then say to these things? If God be for us, who can be against us? ***He that spared not his own Son, but delivered him up for us all, how shall he not with him also freely give us all things?***[15] ***Who shall bring a charge against God's elect? It is God who justifies.***[16] ***Who is he who condemns? It is Christ who died,***[17] and furthermore is also risen, who is even at the right hand of God, who also makes intercession for us. ***Who shall separate us from the love of Christ?***[18] Shall tribulation, or distress, or persecution, or famine, or nakedness, or peril, or sword? As it is written: "For Your sake we are killed all day long; We are accounted as sheep for the slaughter." Yet in all these things we are more than conquerors through Him who loved us. For I am persuaded that neither death nor life, nor angels nor principalities nor powers, nor things present nor things to come, nor height nor depth, nor any other created thing, ***shall be able to separate us from the love of God which is in Christ Jesus our Lord.***[18] **ROMANS 8:31-39**

THE FINISHED WORK OF CHRIST

God is the one who justified us eternally,[16] *so who could possibly condemn us now?*[17] God is the only righteous judge and His judgment is that we are eternally justified through Christ.

Because of this, we have access to all His blessings. *He's not withholding anything from us.*[15] We are more than conquerors in all situations.

Nothing can separate us from the love of God[18] that was displayed in His incredible gift of righteousness through Jesus.

ROMANS 9, 10 AND 11

SUMMARY UNDERSTANDING: These 3 chapters are a parenthetical thought interjected between chapters 8 and 12. The Jews rejected Jesus and *tried to establish their own righteousness by the law.*[19] *They remain ignorant of God's true righteousness by faith.*[20] God's plan is *for them to receive the same mercy*[21] and their eyes will be opened.

> but Israel, pursuing the law of righteousness, has not attained to the law of righteousness. Why? *Because they did not seek it by faith, but as it were, by the works of the law.*[19] For they stumbled at that stumbling stone. As it is written: "Behold, I lay in Zion a stumbling stone and rock of offense, And whoever believes on Him will not be put to shame." ROMANS 9:31-33
>
> Brethren, my heart's desire and prayer to God for Israel is that they may be saved. For I bear them witness that they have a zeal for God, but not according to knowledge. For *they being ignorant of God's righteousness, and seeking to establish their own righteousness, have not submitted to the righteousness of God.*[20] For Christ is the end of the law for righteousness to everyone who believes. ROMANS 10:1-4
>
> I say then, have they stumbled that they should fall? Certainly not! But through their fall, to provoke them to jealousy, salvation has come to the Gentiles. ROMANS 11:11
>
> For as you were once disobedient to God, yet have now obtained mercy through their disobedience, even so these also have now been disobedient, *that through the mercy shown you they also may obtain mercy.*[21] For God has committed them all to disobedience, that He might have mercy on all. ROMANS 11:30-32

ROMANS 12

SUMMARY UNDERSTANDING: After closing the parenthetical thought of chapters 9-11, Paul continues on from the end of chapter 8:

Therefore (since there is no condemnation due to us), it is by God's mercy poured out that we must **present our bodies holy and acceptable**[23] as a **living sacrifice**[22] (not to be killed). In the same way the Old Covenant sacrifice was presented to the priest for inspection and declared holy and acceptable, we too are judged **holy and acceptable**[23] being covered by Jesus perfect sacrifice where He took our condemnation to death upon Himself.

We don't think **according to the way the world thinks,**[25] which sees and judges good and evil (law). We must have our mind **continually renewed**[26] to the fact that salvation is in Christ, not in our self effort to keep the law.

Our **reasonable service,**[24] **or logical way of rendering worship** to God is by calling ourselves the way God sees us—**holy and acceptable by the blood of Christ.**[23] This is how **we prove His perfect will**[27]—it is His plan of redemption, and it is perfect and complete. There's nothing to add. It is finished!

> I beseech you therefore, brethren, by the mercies of God, that you present your bodies a **living sacrifice,**[22] **holy, acceptable**[23] to God, which is your **reasonable service.**[24] And **do not be conformed to this world,**[25] **but be transformed by the renewing of your mind,**[26] **that you may prove what is that good and acceptable and perfect will of God.**[27] ROMANS 12:1-2

ABSORBING DEEPER

1/ What crucial principles does the book of Romans establish?

_____

_____

_____

2/ What are three foundations our Christian faith should be built upon?

_____

_____

_____

3/ **Romans 1:** Why does the unbeliever have no excuse before God?

_____

_____

_____

_____

4/ **Romans 2:** Explain why righteousness cannot be obtained through religious effort.

_____

_____

_____

5/ **Romans 3:** Why are none righteous?

_____

_____

_____

_____

6/ **Romans 4:** How is righteousness reckoned to our account? What is the result of working for righteousness?

_____

_____

_____

7/ **Romans 5:** What is the origin of sin? What is the origin of true righteousness?

_____

_____

_____

8/ **Romans 6:** How has grace freed us from the law?

_____

_____

_____

9/ **Romans 7:** How is being under the law likened to being in a marriage covenant? How are we made free in Christ?

_____

_____

_____

_____

10/**Romans 8:** Why is there no condemnation upon us anymore?

_____

_____

_____

_____

_____

11/Romans 8: What did Paul mean when he said, "do not walk according to the flesh?" What did he mean when he said, "walk according to the Spirit?"

_____

_____

_____

_____

12/Romans 8: What is the foundation of our eternal justification? Who is the judge? What does His judgment give us access to? Can anything separate us from God's provision and favor?

_____

_____

_____

_____

13/Romans 9, 10 and 11: How did the Jews try to establish their own righteousness?

_____

_____

_____

_____

14/Romans 12: How do we present our bodies holy and acceptable before God? What does it mean to present our bodies holy and acceptable?

_____

_____

_____

_____

CHAPTER SEVEN

The New Creation Heart

> But this is the covenant that I will make with the house of Israel after those days, says the LORD: ***I will put My law in their minds, and write it on their hearts;¹*** and I will be their God, and they shall be My people. **JEREMIAH 31:33**

As challenging as it is for our "good and evil" conscious minds to accept, in the New Covenant the pathway to righteous and godly behavior is *not* by trying to keep the law, or by trying to better ourselves, by ourselves in any way. The law is literally the ***ministry of death and condemnation²*** (2 Corinthians 3:7-9). How could we have life by it in any way?

The ministry of righteousness³ is received by faith in the Finished Work of Christ (Chapter 13) and it exceeds in glory so much more. Not only has the Finished Work of Christ made the restoration of Spirit-to-spirit relationship with God the Father a reality, through it, we have been given a new heart with God's law ***written on it¹*** (Jeremiah 31:33).

 This is the ***new birth⁴*** (1 Peter 1:3). It's not a metaphor, but the reality of the New Creation.

> But if ***the ministry of death,²*** written and engraved on stones, was glorious, ... how will the ministry of the Spirit not be more glorious? For if the ***ministry of condemnation²*** had glory, ***the ministry of righteousness³*** exceeds much more in glory. **2 CORINTHIANS 3:7-9**

> Blessed be the God and Father of our Lord Jesus Christ! According to his great mercy, he has caused us to be ***born again⁴*** to a living hope through the resurrection of Jesus Christ from the dead, **1 PETER 1:3 ESV**

Having a new heart, means our spirit man has literally been reborn (Chapter 8). We are completely *new creatures*[5] and we behave entirely different from the old man that had the sin nature (2 Corinthians 5:17).

> Therefore, if anyone is in Christ, he is a *new creation;*[5] old things have passed away; behold, all things have become new. **2 CORINTHIANS 5:17**

KEY GREEK WORD

2937 KTISIS:[5] (ktis'-is) creation (the act or the product), *creature*, institution; always of Divine work.

Even though sin is still at work in our unredeemed flesh and it is possible to give ourselves over to its lusts (Chapter 8 and Romans 7:21-25 p62), we are not sinners with a corrupted sin nature anymore. If we walk according to the flesh, we will end up doing the works of the flesh, but our spirit is man is perfectly redeemed.

> knowing this, that *our old man was crucified with Him,*[6] that the body of sin might be done away with, that *we should no longer be slaves of sin.*[7] *For he who has died has been freed from sin.*[8] Now if we died with Christ, we believe that we shall also live with Him, knowing that Christ, having been raised from the dead, dies no more. Death no longer has dominion over Him. *For the death that He died, He died to sin once for all;*[8] but the life that He lives, He lives to God. *Likewise you also, reckon yourselves to be dead indeed to sin,*[8] but alive to God in Christ Jesus our Lord. Therefore *do not let sin reign in your mortal body*, that you should obey it in its lusts. **ROMANS 6:6-12**

The death we died with Christ was *the death of the old man*[6] and the corrupted sin nature. The stony, rebellious heart was replaced with *the New Creation heart.*[1]

By the Finished Work, we are *free from the penalty of sin.*[8] By the *New Creation heart,*[1] we are *free from the slavery of doing sins.*[7] We can *count ourselves completely dead to sin*[8] (Romans 6:6-12). Now written on our *hearts,*[1] the law has transformed from an impossible "have to," to a Spirit-empowered "want to." The difference between these two states of being is comparable to the contrast between night and day. This is the new reality of being *born again into the New Creation.*[4]

LAW OR GRACE, ONE OR THE OTHER

> Stand fast therefore in the liberty by which Christ has made us free, and **do not be entangled again with a yoke of bondage.**[9] Indeed I, Paul, say to you that if you become circumcised, Christ will profit you nothing. And I testify again to every man who becomes circumcised that he is a debtor to keep the whole law. You have become estranged from Christ, you who attempt to be justified by law; you have **fallen from grace.**[10]
> **GALATIANS 5:1-4**

It is impossible to function in the law and grace at the same time. Some of Paul's greatest **warnings**[9] are about guarding ourselves from the tendency to do self works (Galatians 5:1-4). When we don't understand our **New Creation heart**[1] and our new relationship with the Holy Spirit, this is what we will automatically do since it's all we've ever known.

Even after we have received Christ, having secured our place in eternity with the Lord, it is quite common, to live **fallen from grace**[10] by unknowingly continuing our pattern of self righteous effort. We won't lose our eternal salvation, but leaning on the arm of our flesh, we will be unable to **access God's supernatural provisions of grace by faith;**[11] healing, provision, protection and favor (Romans 5:1-2 and Chapter 5). We'll simply get what the world gets and be subject to the corruption that is still at work in the earth and flesh. To the unsaved, we won't appear much different.

> Therefore, having been justified by faith, we have peace with God through our Lord Jesus Christ, **through whom also we have access by faith into this grace in which we stand,**[11] and rejoice in hope of the glory of God. **ROMANS 5:1-2**

Learning to walk in relationship with the Holy Spirit by faith, is the next step to maturity in Christ. Without it, we'll fall prey to the devil's main MO (Chapters 1 and 2). Forever tempting us to doubt the Word of God, if he succeeds, we will automatically revert to leaning on our own understanding, forever running our lives self-focused in self-reliance. But through the Spirit-empowered life, we will access all that has been provided by the Finished Work of Christ. Study *Speak It:® 30 Days of Saturation in the Spirit-Empowere• Life* for more understanding.

ABSORBING DEEPER

1/ What is challenging for our "good and evil-conscious minds" to accept?

_____

_____

2/ Explain the difference between the ministry of death and condemnation, and the ministry of righteousness?

_____

_____

_____

3/ How does the New Creation heart differ from the heart of an unbeliever? How does it make us behave differently?

_____

_____

_____

_____

4/ What does it mean to be born again, and how is it factual rather than conceptual?

_____

_____

_____

5/ What is the yoke of bondage and how could we be entangled with it again?

_____

_____

_____

6/ How does the yoke of bondage stop us from accessing His grace by faith? How does this relate to the devil's main MO (Chapter 1 and 2)?

_____

_____

_____

_____

_____

7/ Why is self-works and self-reliance our natural tendency?

_____

_____

_____

8/ How do we mature beyond this natural tendency?

_____

_____

_____

9/ Read Romans 7:21-25 on p62. Explain how the law of sin that is at work in the flesh is different from the sin nature of the unredeemed heart? Even being in Christ, explain why we still sin sometimes?

_____

_____

_____

_____

_____

_____

REFLECT AND DISCUSS

10/ In the past, have you understood 2 Corinthians 5:17 as a metaphor? What do you understand now? Explain the night and day difference of being a new creature in Christ. Use your own experiences as a reference.

_____

_____

_____

_____

_____

_____

_____

_____

11/ Recognize some ways you tend to operate in self-reliance. Look up some scriptures that will help you refocus on the provision in the Finished Work. Reflect on these with the Holy Spirit in the moment.

_____

_____

_____

_____

_____

_____

_____

_____

_____

CHAPTER EIGHT

UNDERSTANDING THE NEW MAN

When we receive Christ (Chapter 13) having been born again, each part of our three-part being is in a different state of redemption. 👣 Here is a description of the New Creation man:

1/ Our spirit is completely redeemed[1] and perfected right now.

We were dead and now *we're alive[1]* again to God. We no longer have the corrupted sin nature that is ruled by lust (Ephesians 2:1-3). We have the New Creation heart that *does not want to do sins[3]* (Titus 2:14). We must learn to *put on the new man* and follow the leading of our heart (Colossians 3:10), or we will listen to the unredeemed flesh.

> *And you He made alive,[1] who were dead* in trespasses and sins, *in which you once walked* according to the course of this world, according to the prince of the power of the air, the spirit who now works in the sons of disobedience, among whom also *we all once conducted ourselves in the lusts of our flesh,[2]* fulfilling the desires of the flesh and of the mind, and *were by nature children of wrath, just as the others.* EPHESIANS 2:1-3
>
> who gave Himself for us, that He might redeem us from every lawless deed and purify for Himself His own special people, *zealous for good works.[3]* TITUS 2:14
>
> and have *put on the new man* who is renewed in knowledge according to the image of Him who created him, COLOSSIANS 3:10
>
> The Spirit Himself bears witness with our spirit that we are children of God, ROMANS 8:16

We have been restored to **Spirit-to-spirit relationship with God the Father** (Romans 8:16). Since we were born separated, fellowshipping and perceiving God's perspective and leadership is not as automatic as it was for Adam. We must learn how to purposefully submit ourselves to the leading of the Holy Spirit. This is living and **walking according to the Spirit** (Chapter 6, p48).

2/ _Our soul is in the process of being redeemed_ by the continual renewing of the mind by the Holy Spirit (not by us) (Romans 12:2, Ephesians 4:22-24).

The soul is made up of the mind, will and emotions. Without **the renewing of the mind,** our emotions control us, we make poor decisions based in fear and unbelief, and we automatically speak death instead of life. Many believers stay immature for life and are **destroyed for lack of knowledge** (Hosea 4:6) by falling prey to the devil's constant deceptions in our minds. They remain oppressed living subject to the curse.

Purposefully submitting to renewal of the mind by the Holy Spirit, fellowshipping through the written word of God, we progressively mature in Christ (Colossians 3:1-3).

And do not be conformed to this world, but **be transformed by the renewing of your mind**, that you may prove what is that good and acceptable and perfect will of God. ROMANS 12:2

that you put off, concerning your former conduct, the old man which grows corrupt according to the deceitful lusts, and **be renewed in the spirit of your mind, and that you put on the new man which was created according to God, in true righteousness and holiness.** EPHESIANS 4:22-24

My people are **destroyed for lack of knowledge**.... HOSEA 4:6

If then you were raised with Christ, seek those things which are above, where Christ is, sitting at the right hand of God. **Set your mind on things above, not on things on the earth**. For you died, and your life is hidden with Christ in God. COLOSSIANS 3:1-3

> Therefore, having been justified by faith, we have peace with God through our Lord Jesus Christ, **through whom also we have access by faith into this grace in which we stand,** and rejoice in hope of the glory of God. **ROMANS 5:1-2**

Through learning to access His grace provisions by faith, we will live the Spirit-empowered life, even amongst the corruption that is still in the world and flesh (Romans 5:1-2 and Chapter 5). These include healing, provision, protection, and favor.

3/ _Our body is not yet redeemed_ and the flesh will not be perfected until we see Christ.

Sin and death is a **_law still at work in the flesh_**[4] which wars against the **New Creation heart that wants to do good**[5] (Romans 7:21-25). If we **set our minds on things of the flesh,**[6] we'll live **carnally minded**[7] and give ourselves over to the lust of the flesh (Romans 8:5-6). Still eternally saved, justified and washed by the blood, it's possible to live **according to the flesh,**[8] attempting to keep the law of ourselves (Romans 8:1). This only accentuates the weakness of the flesh and results in works of the flesh.

> I find then **a law, that evil is present with me,**[4] **the one who wills to do good.**[5] For I delight in the law of God according to the inward man. **But I see another law in my members,**[4] **warring against the law of my mind,**[5] and bringing me into captivity to the **law of sin which is in my members.**[4] O wretched man that I am! Who will deliver me from this body of death? I thank God—through Jesus Christ our Lord! So then, with the mind I myself serve the law of God, but with the flesh the law of sin. **ROMANS 7:21-25**
>
> For those who live according to the flesh **set their minds on the things of the flesh,**[6] but those who live according to the Spirit, the things of the Spirit. For **to be carnally minded is death,**[7] but to be spiritually minded is life and peace. **ROMANS 8:5-6**
>
> **There is therefore now no condemnation** to those who are in Christ Jesus, who do not walk **according to the flesh,**[8] but according to the Spirit. **ROMANS 8:1**

No one lives perfectly sinless in Christ. We've had a lifetime of being trained by the nature of the flesh. This is why we need to be washed of all sin, past, present and future. Living focused on the Finished Work of Christ, the lust of the flesh loses its power. We are not slaves to sin, because sin does not exist in our spirit man anymore.

In Christ, there is therefore no condemnation because the sentence of condemnation for sin has been paid for all eternity (Romans 8:1). Walking according to the Spirit is being led by the Holy Spirit and the New Creation heart which empowers us to godly behavior and righteous living.

ABSORBING DEEPER

1/ What are the three parts of our three-part being, and what state of redemption are they each in?

_____

_____

_____

2/ What is the main characteristic of the redeemed spirit man?

_____

_____

_____

_____

3/ In what part of our nature are we restored to God the Father? Why is perceiving our fellowship not as automatic as it was for Adam?

_____

_____

_____

_____

4/ What is the soul made up of?

_____

_____

5/ Who does the renewing of the mind? How can we purposefully submit to this process?

_____

_____

_____

6/ What is the law that is still at work in the flesh and what does it war against?

_____

7/ What is in between the flesh and the spirit? See p61

_____

8/ In your own words, explain the difference between being carnally-minded and spiritually-minded (Romans 8:5-6).

_____

_____

_____

_____

REFLECT AND DISCUSS

9/ Without the Holy Spirit, we make carnal decisions. What are the factors behind this poor decision-making? Think of times you made decisions based on carnal thinking, versus times you made decisions based on fellowship with the Holy Spirit over the Word. What was the difference in results?

_____

_____

_____

_____

_____

_____

_____

_____

_____

CHAPTER NINE

God's Love Poured Out

> But *God demonstrates His own love toward us, in that while we were still sinners, Christ died for us.* Much more then, having now been justified by His blood, we shall be saved from wrath through Him. ROMANS 5:8-9

The Finished Work of Christ is the ultimate picture of the *unfathomable depths of God's love and never-ending mercy.* He did absolutely everything for us. Even while we were lost in sin He provided the way of escape (Romans 5:8-9).

We will keep ourselves in the middle of His amazing love and receive tremendous, never-ending revelation of it by *keeping our eyes fixed on His mercy that was poured out[1]* through the Finished Work (Jude 20-21). He did not come with a wagging finger of *condemnation,[3]* but a desire that we all be *utterly saved[4]* from the pit of death and separation. *Everlasting life in personal, intimate relationship with Him[2]* is His passionate desire for all. He loves each and every one of us *that* personally and *that* deeply, and He gave His only Son, who went willingly all the way to the torturous grave to prove it (John 3:16-17).

> But you, beloved, building yourselves up on your most holy faith, praying in the Holy Spirit, *keep yourselves in the love of God, looking for the mercy of our Lord Jesus Christ[1]* unto eternal life. JUDE 20-21
>
> For God so loved the world that He gave His only begotten Son, that *whoever believes in Him should not perish but have everlasting life.[2]* For *God did not send His Son into the world to condemn the world,[3] but that the world through Him might be saved.[4]* JOHN 3:16-17

Let's summarize before we dive into the details of the Finished Work of Christ:

OUR HOPELESS, CURSED STATE

1. Through Adam's sin, we were separated from God and His original design of creation. We lost God's divine perspective and personal, intimate relationship with Him (Chapter 2).

2. We were born into corruption. Sins are an automatic outpouring of the sin nature (Chapter 3).

3. The knowledge of good and evil is a cursed state of consciousness. It causes us to know, do, and judge both good and evil. We view everything through this lens. It causes self-righteousness and self-driven works (Chapter 2).

4. The earth is cursed along with our flesh, which is born dying, instead of eternal. This is not God's original design (Chapter 2).

5. We are cursed under the law which we cannot keep. The righteous requirement is perfection. The penalty is death (Chapter 4).

6. God's design back to life and personal relationship is through the Finished Work of Christ (Chapters 3 and 4).

7. Everyone must receive salvation by faith in Christ (Chapters 3, 4 and 13).

ABSORBING DEEPER

1/ What is God's greatest demonstration of love towards us and how did He provide the way of escape?

_____

_____

_____

2/ How can we receive deeper revelation of the love of God?

_____

_____

_____

3/ What is God's desire for every single person?

_____

_____

_____

_____

4/ What do you understand differently about our need for our Savior? Do you have a better understanding of God's design of salvation?

_____

_____

_____

_____

_____

_____

CHAPTER TEN

THE FINISHED WORK OF CHRIST

> And you, being dead in your trespasses and the uncircumcision of your flesh, He has made alive together with Him, *having forgiven you all trespasses,¹ having wiped out the handwriting of requirements that was against us,²* which was contrary to us. And *He has taken it out of the way, having nailed it to the cross.³* Having disarmed principalities and powers, He made a public spectacle of them, triumphing over them in it. **COLOSSIANS 2:13-15**

God's plan of redemption is so complete. Nothing was left out. In Jesus' perfect sacrifice, *every sin was forgiven.¹* Even more important, the law that was impossible for us to keep *was wiped out.²* *The handwriting of requirements that was against us² was nailed to the Cross and taken out of the way,³* and *by this,* the devil and all principalities and powers were thoroughly defeated and disarmed (Colossians 2:13-15). 💧 Our sins weren't nailed to the Cross—*the law was,* and this is what defeated the devil for all eternity.

There is more to the Finished Work than the death, burial and resurrection of Jesus. In studying each part of His saving work we'll attempt to understand *the unsearchable riches of Christ,⁴* and help others discover *the fellowship of this mystery⁵* that was hidden from the beginning of the ages.

When we submit to the renewing of our minds to who we are and what we have in Him, we, the church, will be more able to *make known the*

70

> To me, who am less than the least of all the saints, this grace was given, that I should preach among the Gentiles *the unsearchable riches of Christ,*[4] *and to make all see what is the fellowship of the mystery,*[5] which from the beginning of the ages has been hidden in God who created all things through Jesus Christ; to the intent that now *the manifold wisdom of God*[6] *might be made known by the church to the principalities and powers*[7] in the heavenly places, according to the *eternal purpose which He accomplished in Christ Jesus our Lord,*[8] in whom *we have boldness and access with confidence through faith in Him.*[9] EPHESIANS 3:8-12

manifold wisdom of God[6] to others. And we'll rub it in the faces of the *defeated principalities*[7] that have tried to rob us of its power. Unfolding His *eternal purpose in Christ,*[8] we'll *boldly access by faith*[9] all He *accomplished*[8] and help others do the same (Ephesians 3:8-12).

Let's outline each part here:

THE FINISHED WORK OF CHRIST

PART 1:   The Ordination

PART 2:   The Condemnation

PART 3:   The Sentence

         A.   The Whipping Post
         B.   The Crown of Thorns
         C.   The Cross

PART 4:   The Victory

         A.   The Keys
         B.   The Mercy Seat
         C.   The Throne

PART ONE

THE ORDINATION

> When all the people were baptized, it came to pass that Jesus also was baptized; and while He prayed, the heaven was opened. And **the Holy Spirit descended** in bodily form like a dove **upon Him,**[1] and a voice came from heaven which said, **"You are My beloved Son; in You I am well pleased."**[2] Now Jesus Himself **began His ministry**[3] at about thirty years of age,... LUKE 3:21-23

The moment Jesus was baptized by John in the Jordan and the Holy Spirit descended **upon Him**[1] like a dove, was the moment of His ordination and the **endorsement**[2] of the Father (Luke 3:21-23).

But why did Jesus need to be baptized by John's baptism of repentance? He didn't have to repent. **There was no sin in Him**[4] (1 John 3:5).

> And you know that He was manifested to take away our sins, and **in Him there is no sin.**[4]
> 1 JOHN 3:5

FULLY MAN BUT NOT THE SAME

Jesus was fully man but there was a "night-and-day" difference between Him and us.

In Hebrews 4:15 where it says Jesus was "... tempted as we are, **yet without sin,**"[4] we've typically thought that He was challenged by temptation but perfect at not doing sin—an impeccable moral example for us to follow. But this is not the correct understanding of this verse.

> For we do not have a High Priest who cannot sympathize with our weaknesses, but was in all points tempted as we are, **yet without sin.**[4]
> HEBREWS 4:15

Jesus wasn't born of Adam's seed. **He was conceived of the Holy Spirit**[5] (Matthew 1:20-21). Science has now proven that none of the mother's blood passes to the baby, and the blood is the source of life.

So Jesus was born of an incorruptible seed an♦ He was not born of the Adamic bloodline. So being "tempted, *yet without sin,*"[4] means Jesus was completely untainted by the corrupted sin nature. He had a flesh that was made of the same cursed elements of the earth (Chapter 2). But without the corrupted sin nature by which sins are the natural outworking, *He did no sin*[4] (1 Peter 2:22).

> But while he thought about these things, behold, an angel of the Lord appeared to him in a dream, saying, "Joseph, son of David, do not be afraid to take to you Mary your wife, *for that which is conceived in her is of the Holy Spirit.*[5] And she will bring forth a Son, and you shall call His name Jesus, for He will save His people from their sins." MATTHEW 1:20-21

> *"Who committed no sin,*[4] nor was deceit found in His mouth;"
> 1 PETER 2:22

If Jesus had the corrupted nature, He wouldn't have been without blemish and could never have qualified to be the perfect Lamb of God that would take away the sin of the whole world (p104).

THE BAPTISM OF REPENTANCE

<u>When we get baptized</u>, we go down into the water *identifying with the death of Jesus* who paid the price of condemnation for our sin (p103).

<u>When Jesus was baptized</u>, He went down into the water *identifying with our sin and its sentence of death.* Through this act, He acknowledged the purpose of God, declared His willingness to pay the price for all mankind, and accepted the calling to die on our behalf.

THE BAPTISM OF THE HOLY SPIRIT

Having been born of the Holy Spirit, Jesus was *filled* from birth. But in Luke 3:21-23, when the Holy Spirit descended like a dove, Jesus received the *anointing of the Holy Spirit upon Him.*[1]

A perfect picture of the *two different applications of the Holy Spirit* (Chapter 13), this moment describes the baptism of the Holy Spirit. This essential topic is covered in detail in *Speak It:® 30 Days of Saturation in the Spirit-Empowere♦ Life.*

> how God **anointed Jesus of Nazareth with the Holy Spirit[1] and with power,[7]** who went about doing good and healing all who were oppressed by the devil, for God was with Him. ACTS 10:38

It's important to note that it wasn't until this crucial juncture, when Jesus received the **power[7] of the Holy Spirit upon Him,[1]** that **His entire ministry began[3]** (Luke 3:23, Acts 10:38).

Moving forward from this pivotal moment, everything changed. Luke 4 starts with Jesus, being **filled[6]** with the Holy Spirit, or rather **completed[6]** with both applications—the **indwelling and the enduing upon.[1]**

He was driven into the desert to be tested by the devil. After prevailing, He returned **in the power[7] of the Spirit[1]** to Galilee (Luke 4:14).

Then He walked into the temple and boldly declared He was the fulfillment of Isaiah 61, and He read the scroll which was a prophecy about Himself.

KEY GREEK WORD

4134 PLÉRÉS:[6] (play'-race) full, abounding in, **complete,** completely occupied with.

> Then Jesus, being **filled[6]** with the Holy Spirit, returned from the Jordan and was led by the Spirit into the wilderness, LUKE 4:1

> Then Jesus **returned in the power[7] of the Spirit[1]** to Galilee,... LUKE 4:14

Recorded here in Luke 4:18-19, it describes everything Jesus came to do in His ministry calling. How would He do it? Not of Himself, but by the **power[7] and anointing of the Holy Spirit[1]**—"**The Spirit of the Lord is upon me,[1] because He has anointed me...**"

> "The Spirit of the Lord is **upon Me,[1]** because He has **anointed[1]** Me to preach the gospel to the poor; He has sent Me to heal the brokenhearted, to proclaim liberty to the captives and recovery of sight to the blind, to set at liberty those who are oppressed; to proclaim the acceptable year of the Lord." LUKE 4:18-19

AUTHORIZED AND EMPOWERED SONSHIP

Now let's return to Jesus' baptism in Luke 3:21-23. In the same moment the Holy Spirit descended *upon Him,[1]* the Father gave Jesus His endorsement. God declared *"this is my beloved Son, in whom I am well pleased."[2]*

Along with the *dunamis[7] miracle-working power[7]* from on high, this acknowledgment came with *the delegation of God's exousia[8] authority*. Jesus was now the *authorized[8] and empowered[7] Son of God.* The Father *approved Him[2]* and *set His seal upon Him[2]* (John 6:27). Everything He did from this moment on had the *power[7]* and *authority[8]* of heaven behind it.

> ## KEY GREEK WORD
>
> **1411 DUNAMIS:**[7] (doo'-nam-is) miraculous power, might, strength
>
> **1849 EXOUSIA:**[8] (ex-oo-see'-ah) power to act, authority † delegated empowerment, delegated authority, refers to the authority God gives to His saints authorizing them to act to the extent they are guided by faith (His revealed word).

> Do not labor for the food which perishes, but for the food which endures to everlasting life, which the Son of Man will give you, because God the Father has *set His seal on Him."[2]* JOHN 6:27

Jesus was strengthened and *empowered[7] by the Holy Spirit[1]* and carried this anointing through His three-year earthly ministry, all the way to the Cross, and to the Throne.

WE ARE AUTHORIZED AND EMPOWERED SONS

> So Jesus said to them again, "Peace to you! *As the Father has sent Me, I also send you."* And when He had said this, He breathed on them, and said to them, "Receive the Holy Spirit." JOHN 20:21–22

In the same way the Father sent Jesus, so He sent us (John 20:21-22). Not only His disciples, but every believer has been *commanded*[9] *to receive the same enduring upon*[1] *of the Holy Spirit* (Acts 1:4-5 and Chapter 13). It's not a suggestion!

In fact, the very reason Jesus became a curse for us is made clear in Galatians 3:13-14. It wasn't only for us to be eternally justified and restored to personal relationship. It was *so that*[10] the blessing of Abraham (eternal justification, see Chapter 5) would come upon us, *so that*[10] we could qualify to receive *the Promise of the Father,*[1] which is the *empowerment*[7] *of the Holy Spirit.*[1]

> And being assembled together with them, *He commanded them*[9] not to depart from Jerusalem, but to wait for *the Promise of the Father*[1] "which," He said, "you have heard from Me; for John truly baptized with water, *but you shall be baptized with the Holy Spirit*[1] not many days from now." **ACTS 1:4-5**

> Christ has redeemed us from the curse of the law, having become a curse for us (for it is written, "Cursed is everyone who hangs on a tree"), *that*[10] the blessing of Abraham might come upon the Gentiles in Christ Jesus, *that*[10] we might receive *the promise of the Spirit*[1] through faith. **GALATIANS 3:13-14**
>
> For as many as are led by the Spirit of God, *these are sons*[11] *of God.* **ROMANS 8:14**
>
> But you shall *receive power*[7] *when the Holy Spirit has come upon*[1] *you;* and you shall be witnesses to Me in Jerusalem, and in all Judea and Samaria, and to the end of the earth." **ACTS 1:8**

Our conversion from sons of Adam to *authorized*[8] *and empowered*[7] *sons*[11] of God is meant to bear witness to His resurrection to the ends of the earth (Romans 8:14, Acts 1:8).

ABSORBING DEEPER

1/ What is the difference between Jesus and us?

_____

_____

_____

_____

2/ Since Jesus had no sin, what was He identifying with, and agreeing to, when He went into the water at the baptism of John?

_____

_____

_____

_____

3/ What are the two different applications of the Holy Spirit?

_____

_____

_____

4/ What comes with the Baptism of the Holy Spirit? See Acts 1:8.

_____

_____

_____

5/ What changed when Jesus received the Baptism of the Holy Spirit?

_____

_____

_____

_____

6/ What words did God speak that were His endorsement and ordination of Jesus?

_____

_____

7/ What else, besides dunamis power, did God anoint Jesus with?

_____

_____

8/ What does John 20:21-22 say about how we are equipped and sent?

_____

_____

_____

9/ What is the promise of the Father?

_____

_____

REFLECT AND DISCUSS

10/ Referring to Galatians 3:13-14, can you see the reason Jesus became a curse for us? Beyond securing our place in heaven, there is a greater reason for being empowered by the Holy Spirit. Why are we given the same endorsement?

_____

_____

_____

_____

_____

_____

PART TWO

The Condemnation

> But the chief priests and elders persuaded the multitudes that they should ask for Barabbas and destroy Jesus. The governor answered and said to them, "Which of the two do you want me to release to you?" They said, "Barabbas!"
>
> Pilate said to them, "What then shall I do with Jesus who is called Christ?" They all said to him, "Let Him be crucified!" **MATTHEW 27:20-22**

Not wanting to be guilty themselves, the Jewish chief priests and elders devised the way for Jesus to be killed. Having committed no crime, He was handed over to Pilate to be judged.

Inciting a multitude to anger, they mounted fierce pressure upon the Roman governor and demanded He be crucified. Caving in to the influence of the crowds, Pilate eventually gave the final judgment and condemned Jesus to be crucified (Matthew 27:20-22).

Back in John 10:18, knowing exactly all these things that awaited Him, Jesus declared that the power to lay down his life and take it up again was His own. Following the command of the Father, He made the choice to be obedient to the calling.

> No one takes it from Me, but I lay it down of Myself. I have power to lay it down, and I have power to take it again. This command I have received from My Father." **JOHN 10:18**

> Or do you think that I cannot now pray to My Father, and He will provide Me with more than twelve legions of angels? How then could the Scriptures be fulfilled, that it must happen thus?" **MATTHEW 26:53-54**
>
> For He made Him who knew no sin to be sin for us, that we might become the righteousness of God in Him. **2 CORINTHIANS 5:21**
>
> The next day he saw Jesus coming to him and said, "Behold, the Lamb of God who takes away the sin of the world! **JOHN 1:29**

Then later in Gethsemane as the guards came to arrest Him, He proclaimed He had the ability to just pray the Father and be saved by legions of angels (Matthew 26:53-54).

But knowing no sin (2 Corinthians 5:21), as the crowds mocked and jeered, and Pilate handed down the death sentence, Jesus gave Himself completely. He became our scapegoat, the perfect Lamb of God who took upon Himself the sins of the whole world. He willingly accepted *the condemnation that was upon us and took it upon Himself* (John 1:29).

ABSORBING DEEPER

1/ How do we know it was Jesus' decision to take the condemnation of all mankind upon Himself?

_____

_____

_____

_____

2/ So if Jesus' condemnation was the plan of God, who were merely the instruments to carry it out?

_____

_____

_____

_____

REFLECT AND DISCUSS

3/ Why do you think Jesus didn't call on legions of angels to save Him?

_____

_____

_____

4/ What did Jesus completely agree to and give Himself for?

_____

_____

_____

_____

PART THREE

The Sentence

> But He was wounded for our transgressions, He was bruised for our iniquities; the chastisement for our peace was upon Him, and **by His stripes we are healed.**[1] ISAIAH 53:5

The sentence of condemnation had three components to it and each covered and sanctified a different part of our three-part being. The Whipping Post covered our body and flesh; the Crown of Thorns covered our soul; and the Cross covered our spirit.

As we study each of the three torturous elements of the sentence, we will come to understand **_the great exchange_** that Jesus made for us **_in each area._**

A. THE WHIPPING POST

THE SENTENCE PAID FOR OUR BODY AND FLESH

Jesus bore stripes **_in exchange_** for our health and healing. The end of Isaiah 53:5 is clear. **_...by His stripes we are healed._**[1]

So many examples of Jesus' life and ministry prove that this **_healing_**[1] is physical and cannot be construed as spiritual, as some have suggested. Here are just a few proofs:

The shedding of blood on the Cross caused our spirit man to be completely redeemed and reborn (Chapter 8, p60).

How could our spirit need healing when it is perfect already? Healing happens nowhere in the spirit man.

The soul requires the renewing of the mind, not healing, to be restored and redeemed. (Chapter 8, p61).

Matthew 8:16-17 connects Isaiah 53:5 and Jesus *healing of the sick*.[1]

In Matthew 10:8, Jesus commissioned His disciples to *heal the sick*,[1] and in Mark 16:17-18, declared the same to *all who believe*. The ministry of laying hands *on the sick*[1] is for every believer, from those present at the time, to us today, and those of the future.

IT'S ALREADY DONE

According to the past tense used in 1 Peter 2:24, which is another direct reference to Isaiah 53:5, we *were healed*[1] over 2,000 years ago. Being trained by a linear timeline since birth, our natural mind is challenged to comprehend this fact. It's especially true when we see sickness and decay all around with our natural eyes, even amongst fellow saints and those who profess to believe. How could our *healing*[1] already be completed, and at the same time, symptoms exist?

In the same way that Jesus secured our salvation over 2,000 years ago, we didn't

> When evening had come, they brought to Him many who were demon-possessed. And He cast out the spirits with a word, and *healed all who were sick*,[1] that it might be fulfilled which was spoken by Isaiah the prophet, saying: "He Himself took our infirmities and bore our *sicknesses*."[1] MATTHEW 8:16-17
>
> *Heal the sick*,[1] cleanse the lepers, raise the dead, cast out demons. Freely you have received, freely give. MATTHEW 10:8
>
> And these signs will follow those *who believe*: In My name they will cast out demons; they will speak with new tongues; they will take up serpents; and if they drink anything deadly, it will by no means hurt them; *they will lay hands on the sick*,[1] *and they will recover*." MARK 16:17-18
>
> who Himself bore our sins in His own body on the tree, that we, having died to sins, might live for righteousness—by whose stripes *you were healed*.[1] 1 PETER 2:24

appropriate it until we believed and received. The only difference between *healing*[1] and salvation is that once we receive salvation our spirit man is perfectly redeemed once and for all. Conversely, corruption still exists in the flesh and we won't receive the completed redemption of our body until the resurrection (Chapter 8, p62). ⬤ So healing is something we must **continually access and receive by faith** to hold off sickness and slow down the continual corruption that is at work in the flesh.

Appropriating the *healing*[1] that has already been completed by His stripes at the Whipping Post is a lengthy topic. There are many aspects to understand and the devil has exploited our lack of understanding since the beginning. But we must seek continual revelation in fellowship with the Holy Spirit. *Speak It:*® *30 Days of Saturation in Healing* is a great in-depth resource to study and receive biblically based revelation.

But in short, we have been called to walk by faith in the Word of God, not by sight (2 Corinthians 5:7). We can't base our faith on other people's experiences or even our own. It's impossible to know what another person truly believes or what strongholds exist. The only truth we can go by is the truth of the Word of God that is forever settled in heaven (Psalm 119:89).

> For we walk by faith, not by sight.
> **2 CORINTHIANS 5:7**
>
> Forever, O LORD, Your word is settled in heaven. **PSALM 119:89**

THE LINK BETWEEN FORGIVENESS AND HEALING

Death and sickness in the body is part of the curse that came from the fall of man (Chapter 2). Through the Finished Work, Jesus saved us from the curse, and forgiveness of sins that came from the sin nature is one of the main components.

Throughout scripture, physical *healing,*[1] ceremonial cleansing and forgiveness of sins are repeatedly and inextricably linked. Here are just a few examples: Mark 1:40-42, James 5:15, and Psalm 103:3, Matthew 9:2-7.

Now a leper came ... saying to Him, "If You are willing, You can make me clean." Then Jesus ... said to him, "I am willing; be cleansed." As soon as He had spoken, immediately the leprosy left him, and he was cleansed. **MARK 1:40–42**

And the prayer of faith will save the sick, and the Lord will raise him up. And if he has committed sins, he will be forgiven. **JAMES 5:15**

...Who forgives all your iniquities, Who heals all your diseases,.. **PSALM 103:3**

Then behold, they brought to Him a paralytic lying on a bed. When Jesus saw their faith, He said to the paralytic, "Son, be of good cheer; your sins are forgiven you." And at once some of the scribes said within themselves, "This Man blasphemes!" But Jesus, knowing their thoughts, said, "Why do you think evil in your hearts? For which is easier, to say, 'Your sins are forgiven you,' or to say, 'Arise and walk'? But that you may know that the Son of Man has power on earth to forgive sins"— then He said to the paralytic, "Arise, take up your bed, and go to your house." And he arose and departed to his house. **MATTHEW 9:2-7**

Where there is forgiveness of sins, *healing*[1] is possible. In fact, frequently Jesus declared a person's forgiveness, then immediately healed them. Without forgiveness of sins, the curse has a cause

Like a flitting sparrow, like a flying swallow, so a curse without cause shall not alight. **PROVERBS 26:2**

to come upon us (Proverbs 26:2). But when the cause for the curse has been removed, there is no longer a judicial cause for sickness.

TAKING PART OF THE FUTURE PROMISE

Before Jesus carried out the work of salvation, Old Covenant saints were able to take part of the future promise of salvation by carrying out the ordinances of the temple. Through sacrifices and washings, they put faith in, and acted upon the shadows and types and received salvation for a full year. Certainly not the fullness of what we are blessed with in the New Covenant; even so, they had salvation by faith.

There are two ordinances in the New Covenant; Baptism and Communion. In the same way, even though the full redemption of the flesh is in our future, through the ordinance of Communion, we can take part of the future promise of the perfected flesh now! Jesus removed the legal right for death and sickness to exist in our body. By putting faith in the ordinance and seeking revelation understanding that causes faith to arise, we can access **healing**[1] and divine health in our body now.

THE ORDINANCE OF COMMUNION

24 and when He had given thanks, He broke it and said, "Take, eat; this is My body which is broken for you; do this in remembrance of Me." *25* In the same manner He also took the cup after supper, saying, "This cup is the new covenant in My blood. This do, as often as you drink it, in remembrance of Me." *26* For as often as you eat this bread and drink this cup, you proclaim the Lord's death till He comes. *27* Therefore whoever eats this bread or drinks this cup of the Lord *in an unworthy manner*[2] will be *guilty*[3] of the body and blood of the Lord. *28* But let a man *examine*[4] himself, and *so*[5] let him eat of the bread and drink of the cup. *29* For he who *eats and drinks*[6] in *an unworthy manner*[2] *eats and drinks*[6] *judgment*[7] to himself, not *discerning*[8] the Lord's body. *30 For this reason*[9] many are weak and sick *among you,*[10] and many sleep. *1 CORINTHIANS 11:24-30*

1 Corinthians 11:24-30 is one of the most well-known passages on Communion. It's also an example of one of the most incorrect and misleading translations from the original Greek into English. The misunderstanding of this scripture is responsible for one of the most harmful doctrines to appropriating grace by faith.

But it's not surprising, since from the beginning, the devil has tried to corrupt our perception of salvation so we don't walk in its power. Even though the devil is a defeated foe, in this dispensation, he is the ruler of this age. The correct understanding of this passage is way too powerful and harmful to his kingdom.

So let's carefully analyze it referring to the original text.

In verse 27 is a stern warning;

> Therefore whoever eats this bread or drinks this cup of the Lord **in an unworthy manner**[2] will be guilty of the body and blood of the Lord.
> **1 CORINTHIANS 11:27**

It immediately sounds so foreboding. But as we consider what comes next, let's keep in mind that our **guilt**[3] is exactly what the Finished Work paid for—the price that we couldn't pay.

Now, before attempting to discern what **an unworthy manner**[2] is, verse 28 actually tells us exactly what **a worthy manner**[5] is.

The Greek word 3779 HOUTÓ[5] means, **in this manner.**[5] Obviously, since the preceding verse talks about **an unworthy manner,**[2] rather than translating this word as **"so,"** the best choice is clearly **"in this manner."**[4]

> **KEY GREEK WORDS**
>
> 3779 **HOUTÓ**:[5] (hoo'-to) in this way, thus, so, **in this manner.**
>
> 1381 **DOKIMAZO**:[4] (dok-im-ad'-zo) to test, by implication to approve

Now verse 27 and 28 should read:

> Therefore whoever eats this bread or drinks this cup of the Lord **in an unworthy manner**[2] will be **guilty**[3] of the body and blood of the Lord. But let a man **examine**[4] himself, and **in this manner,**[5] let him eat of the bread and drink of the cup.

What a difference that makes to understanding this scripture already!

The next word to look at is 1381 DOKIMAZO,[4] which was translated as **examine,**[4] but according to the definition from Strong's Concordance, the fuller meaning of this word is **to test and by implication, to approve.**

What is the *only way* we could possibly **test, and by implication, approve**[4] ourselves? Only by the blood of Christ are we **approved.**[4] So testing and seeing ourselves **approved**[4] by the blood of Christ is clearly the **worthy manner**[5] by which we should **eat this bread and drink this cup!** After all, isn't remembering and acknowledging our eternal justification by His sacrifice exactly what taking communion is all about?

In fact, if the implication of the English translation was correct, wouldn't we be doing exactly the opposite of what the Finished Work did for us? We would be judging ourselves by our good and evil consciousness, according to the law, and we would be guilty. No one could take Communion in a worthy manner, *ever!*

If that wasn't enough, verse 29 is the worst part of this mistranslation:

The English repeats the phrase, *in an unworthy manner,*[2] yet in the Greek it is not repeated.

Noting the word for *judgment,*[7] 2917 KRIMA,[7] an adverse judgment or a condemnation, and the word for *discerning,* 1252 DIAKRINÓ,[8] to distinguish and separate one thing from another, let's translate this whole verse more accurately:

KEY GREEK WORDS

2917 KRIMA:[7] (kree'-mah) a judgment, a verdict; sometimes implying an adverse verdict, a condemnation.

1252 DIAKRINÓ:[8] (dee-ak-ree'-no) from dia—*separate*, and 2919 KRÍNŌ—judge, to distinguish, to judge, *separate, down the middle, distinguish, discern one thing from another;* decide.

> The one who *eats and drinks*[6] *an adverse judgment*[7] on himself, is the one who *eats and drinks*[6] not *distinguishing*[8] *and separating*[8] the body (from the blood).

This correct translation changes our understanding of the scripture entirely. Now, in verse 30, Paul sums up like this:

> *For this reason*[9] many are weak and sick *among you,*[10] and many *sleep.*[11]

For this reason,[9] not *a* reason!

Not distinguishing[8] the bread from the wine, the body from the blood, *is the reason*[9] many *among us*[10] get sick and die when we don't have to.

KEY GREEK WORD

2837 KOIMAÓ:[11] (koy-mah'-o) sleep, die

The scourging of the Lord's body at the Whipping Post was for healing, and the shedding of blood on the Cross was for forgiveness of sins.

Clearly distinguishing between healing and forgiveness of sins is *rightly dividing*[8] the *word*[12] of truth, and Jesus and His Finished Work *is* that *Word*[12] (2 Timothy 2:15)!

> Study to present yourself approved to God, a worker who does not need to be ashamed, *rightly dividing*[8] *the word*[12] *of truth*. 2 TIMOTHY 2:15 KJV

Now, let's read 1 Corinthians 11:24-30 with the correct understanding:

> and when He had given thanks, He broke it and said, "Take, eat; this is My body which is broken for you; do this in remembrance of Me." In the same manner He also took the cup after supper, saying, "This cup is the new covenant in My blood. This do, as often as you drink it, in remembrance of Me." For as often as you eat this bread and drink this cup, you proclaim the Lord's death till He comes. Therefore whoever eats this bread or drinks this cup of the Lord *in an unworthy manner*[2] will be guilty of the body and blood of the Lord. But let a man *test, and by implication approve*[4] himself *(washed by the blood),* and *in this manner,*[5] let him eat of the bread and drink of the cup. The one who *eats and drinks*[6] *an adverse judgment*[7] on himself, is the one who *eats and drinks*[6] *not distinguishing*[8] *and separating*[8] the body *(from the blood). For this reason*[9] many are weak and sick *among you,*[10] and many die.

The clarity of this passage and its intended meaning is undeniable!

BEATING NOT REQUIRED FOR ETERNAL SALVATION

No animal sacrifices in the temple were ever beaten. Jesus didn't have to take the beating at the Whipping Post for us to be eternally saved. But He did so we could take part of the future promise of our redeemed and perfected flesh. His body <u>exchanged</u> for ours, so we could have healing, here and now.

HEALING IN THE BREAD OF LIFE

The manna that rained down upon the children of Israel in Exodus 16 was merely the shadow. Jesus is the substance and the true *Bread*[13] *of Life*[14] (John 6:51).

> I am *the living bread*[13] *which came down from heaven*. If anyone eats of this *bread,*[13] he will live forever; and the *bread*[13] that I shall give is My flesh, which I shall give for the *life*[14] of the world JOHN 6:51

Being a perfect nutrition source, the supernatural provision of manna was not only food, it supplied health. None died on the journey from Egypt to the Promised Land, even amongst their grumbling and complaining, even in their unbelief. The law had not yet been given and so they were covered by grace and kept in divine health.

> Then they said to Him, "What shall we do, that we may work the works of God?" Jesus answered and said to them, "This is the work of God, that you believe in Him whom He sent." JOHN 6:28-29
>
> Then Jesus said to them, "Most assuredly, I say to you, Moses did not give you the *bread*[13] from heaven, but My Father gives you the *true bread*[13] *from heaven*. For the *bread*[13] of God is He who comes down from heaven and gives *life*[14] to the world." Then they said to Him, "Lord, give us this *bread*[13] always." And Jesus said to them, *"I am the bread*[13] *of life.*[14] He who comes to Me shall never hunger, and he who believes in Me shall never thirst. JOHN 6:32-35

In John 6, Jesus declares Himself as the *Bread*[13] *of Life*[14] — ZÓÉ[14] life! Amongst its definitions in Thayer's Greek Lexicon, 2222 ZÓÉ[14] is described as life preserved in

KEY GREEK WORD

2222 ZÓÉ:[14] (dzo-ay') life. Life preserved in the midst of perils, with a suggestion of vigor and absolute fullness of life.

the midst of perils, with a suggestion of vigor and absolute fullness of life. Doesn't this definition clearly describe how we receive health and healing amid the sickness of the corrupted world and flesh?

HEALING IS IN THE CHILDREN'S BREAD

The Syro-Phoenician woman in Matthew 15:24-28 begged Jesus to heal her demon-possessed daughter. In response, Jesus essentially

> But He answered and said, "I was not sent except to the lost sheep of the house of Israel." Then she came and worshiped Him, saying, "Lord, help me!" But He answered and said, "It is not good to take *the children's bread*[13] and throw it to the little dogs." And she said, "Yes, Lord, yet even the little dogs eat the crumbs which fall from their masters' table." Then Jesus answered and said to her, "O woman, great is your faith! Let it be to you as you desire." And her daughter was *healed*[1] from that very hour. MATTHEW 15:24-28

termed Himself as *the children's bread*[13] that would bring *healing,*[1] and He, the *Bread*[13] *of Life,*[14] was only there for the children of Israel.

Of course He honored her bold faith with *healing.*[1] Even this non-Jewish woman recognized the Messiah and she received of the *Bread*[13] *of Life*[14] for her daughter.

MEDITATE

As we eat of the *bread*[13] in Communion, remembering His body given for our *healing,*[1] all of these references to the *Bread*[13] *of* ZÓÉ *Life,*[14] are perfect to meditate on. In fellowship with the Holy Spirit, He will cause faith to arise by revelation and we will take hold of the *healing*[1] He provided at the Whipping Post.

Study *Speak It:*® *30 Days of Saturation in Healing* to go deeper into the biblical principles of *healing*[1] by faith.

ABSORBING DEEPER

1/ What are the three parts to the sentence and what part of our three-part being does each cover?

_____

_____

_____

2/ What was *the great exchange* in the Whipping Post?

_____

_____

_____

_____

3/ What is one proof that Isaiah 53:5 refers to physical healing?

_____

_____

_____

4/ What is the difference between Isaiah 53:5 and 1 Peter 2:24?

_____

_____

_____

5/ How can healing be already done, yet symptoms exist? How does it compare to the salvation of our spirit man and how is it different?

_____

_____

_____

_____

6/ How can we access healing, even though our flesh is still in a corrupted state? HINT: 2 Corinthians 5:7 and Romans 5:2. Support your answer with another scripture that is an example of what God says on the subject of healing.

_____

_____

_____

_____

7/ What is the link between forgiveness and healing? What is one scripture that makes this connection obvious?

_____

_____

_____

_____

8/ In your own words, use Proverbs 26:2 to explain why sickness has no legal right to be in your body.

_____

_____

_____

_____

9/ Explain what it means to take part in the future promise of our perfected flesh. How is this possible and what is the biblical precedent?

_____

_____

_____

_____

10/What is the worthy manner in which we should take Communion?

_____

_____

_____

11/What is **the** reason many among us are sick and die even though Jesus took stripes for our healing?

_____

_____

_____

12/What's the difference between the bread and the wine?

_____

_____

_____

13/How is the manna that rained down from heaven in Exodus 16 a shadow of Jesus? What are some of the parallel pictures?

_____

_____

_____

_____

_____

_____

_____

_____

REFLECT AND DISCUSS

14/Take Communion and write how each element applies to you today. For example, as you take the bread, declare what Jesus' body has done for any symptoms you may be experiencing. Take the juice and thank God for the forgiveness of sins, remembering what you were saved from.

_____

_____

_____

_____

_____

_____

_____

_____

_____

_____

_____

_____

_____

_____

_____

_____

_____

_____

B. THE CROWN OF THORNS

THE SENTENCE PAID FOR OUR SOUL

> Then the soldiers of the governor took Jesus into the Praetorium and gathered the whole garrison around Him. And they stripped Him and put a scarlet robe on Him. When they had twisted *a crown of thorns,*[1] they put it on His head, and a reed in His right hand. And they bowed the knee before Him and mocked Him, saying, "Hail, King of the Jews!" Then they spat on Him, and took the reed and struck Him on the head. And when they had mocked Him, they took the robe off Him, put His own clothes on Him, and led Him away to be crucified. **MATTHEW 27:27-31**

So often overlooked and underestimated, the **Crown of Thorns**[1] was a savage incident far beyond the quick description in Matthew 27:27-31.

The King of kings who deserves all glory and honor, instead received the **Crown of Thorns.**[1] Making brutal mockery of Him, they stripped Him naked and put Him to utter shame. But little did they know, in this callous moment, Jesus willingly bore the cursed, fallen thinking of the whole world **in exchange** that we could have the mind of Christ through the leadership of the Holy Spirit (1 Corinthians 2:12-16 p99).

Let's understand by looking at a few shadows and types, especially focusing on the **thorns.**[1]

THE FRUITFUL OR CURSED GROUND OF THE HEART

There are two important scriptures that reference **thorns:**[1]

> ..."Cursed is the **ground**[2] for your sake; in toil you shall eat of it all the days of your life. Both **thorns**[1] and thistles it shall bring forth for you...
> **GENESIS 3:17-18**

❶ The first time **thorns**[1] are mentioned in the Bible is at the pronouncement of **the curse upon the ground**[2] when the earth became unfruitful (Genesis 3:17-18). Now it would only produce by their hard work. In contrast, before the curse, the ground was exceedingly abundant and fruitful.

> Now the **ones**[3] that fell among **thorns**[1] are those who, when they have heard, go out and are choked with **cares,**[4] riches, and pleasures of life, and bring **no fruit to maturity**[5]... LUKE 8:14

The second scripture we'll look at that has an important reference to **thorns**[1] is the parable of the sower of the seed (Luke 8:14).

First, let's note the pictures and their representational meanings:

Thorns[1] represent **unfruitfulness.**[5]

The **ground**[2] represents the **heart**[2] of man.

The **seed**[3] is the **Word of God**[3] that is being planted into man's **hearts**[2] **(the ground**[2]**)**.

The **seed**[3] that falls among the **thorns**[1] is the **word**[3] that is **unfruitful**[5] and brings **no fruit to maturity**[5]

The **Word of God**[3] successfully planted deep in our **heart**[2] transforms us from the inside out. As the Holy Spirit causes correct understanding, the **Word**[3] takes root and produces **fruitful** thinking and faith-filled, Spirit-led actions that affect all aspects of our life.

On the other hand, the **Word of God**[3] that is choked by **cares,**[4] riches and pleasures of the world is hindered from being rooted in our **hearts**[2] (Luke 8:14). This carnal thinking based in self-reliance shuts out the voice of the Holy Spirit and causes the **Word**[3] to be **unfruitful**[5] in our life.

Shown in the definition of the word 3308 MERIMNA,[4] worry and anxiety is the underlying problem of a person who is chasing after riches and pleasures. Fear of lack is just one example of **cursed thinking**. Void of faith and without understanding of the provision in **the Finished Work,**[3] this mindset propels us into self works and hinders us from entering into the Spirit-led relationship.

KEY GREEK WORD

3308 MERIMNA:[4] **worry, anxiety**. From merízō, "divide," separated from the whole; worry (anxiety), dividing and fracturing a person's being into parts.

Instead, when we are not secure in His provision, we try to do and even pray for what he's already provided. We live looking to our own ability (pride) or inability (fear). Either way, the result is the same. We're subject to the **cursed, unfruitful,⁴ thorny¹ ground²** of the heart where the **Word³** cannot take root and **does not produce⁴** what it is supposed to (Chapter 2).

> And my God shall supply all your need according to His riches in glory by Christ Jesus. **PHILIPPIANS 4:19**
>
> **Be anxious for nothing**, but in everything by prayer and supplication, with thanksgiving, **let your requests be made known to God**; and the peace of God, which surpasses all understanding, will guard your hearts and minds through Christ Jesus. **PHILIPPIANS 4:6-7**
>
> casting all your care upon Him, **for He cares for you**. 1 PETER 5:7
>
> The blessing of the Lord makes one rich, and He adds no sorrow with it. **PROVERBS 10:22**

In contrast, a person whose mind is focused in faith on the **Word of God³** will be abundantly **fruitful**, able to lay hold of all the promises of His provision. This highlights how crucial it is to study and meditate on **His Word.³** Here are just a few examples of what we should do with the cares of the world (Philippians 4:19, Philippians 4:6-7, 1 Peter 5:7).

Granted, the world can get pretty good results from natural effort *some of the time*. But natural effort can only produce natural results, and how much sorrow comes with it (Proverbs 10:22)?

In contrast, living the Spirit-empowered life that Jesus' Finished Work provided always produces **exceedingly beyond all we could ever imagine** (Ephesians 3:20).

> Now to Him who is able to do **exceedingly abundantly above all that we ask or think**, according to the power that works in us, EPHESIANS 3:20

THE CROWN OF THORNS FOR THE MIND OF CHRIST

By enduring this excruciating part of the sentence, Jesus bore all the things that go with the cursed mind, including our shame, condemnation and the torment of not being at peace with God.

Furthermore, through the Finished Work, there is no more enmity between us and God the Father. We have received the Spirit and have **direct access to God** (Ephesians 2:16-18).

◉ Through this relationship, it's possible for us to actually **know all things** (1 John 2:20) and have the wisdom of God. This completely new way of thinking and viewing our life is true spiritual discernment. Our whole relationship with the Holy Spirit is a learning relationship. It's Him that teaches us and we must submit and position ourselves to learn.

Without the Holy Spirit, the world cannot discern spiritual things. But just like Adam did before the fall, now it's possible for us to discern the world through God's eyes (Chapter 2). Being intimately acquainted once again, we have God's perspective—we have **the mind of Christ** (1 Corinthians 2:12-16).

> and that He might reconcile them both to God in one body through the cross, thereby **putting to death the enmity.** And He came and preached peace to you who were afar off and to those who were near. **For through Him we both have access by one Spirit to the Father.** EPHESIANS 2:16-18
>
> But you have an anointing from the Holy One, and **you know all things.** 1 JOHN 2:20
>
> Now we have received, not the spirit of the world, but the Spirit who is from God, **that we might know the things that have been freely given to us by God.** These things we also speak, not in words which man's wisdom teaches but which the Holy Spirit teaches, comparing spiritual things with spiritual. **But the natural man does not receive the things of the Spirit of God, for they are foolishness to him; nor can he know them, because they are spiritually discerned.** But he who is spiritual judges all things, yet he himself is rightly judged by no one. For "who has known the mind of the Lord that he may instruct Him?" **But we have the mind of Christ.** 1 CORINTHIANS 2:12-16

So through setting our minds on spiritual things and developing our relationship under the learning yoke of the Holy Spirit, the carnal mind that produces the cursed thinking of the world loses its hold. This spiritual mind produces life and peace (Romans 8:5-7).

For those who live according to the flesh set their minds on the things of the flesh, but those who live according to the Spirit, the things of the Spirit. For to be carnally minded is death, but ***to be spiritually minded is life and peace.*** Because the carnal mind is enmity against God; for it is not subject to the law of God, nor indeed can be. **ROMANS 8:5-7**

Grace and peace be multiplied to you in the ***knowledge*** of God and of Jesus our Lord, as His divine power has given to us all things that pertain to life and godliness, through the knowledge of Him who called us by glory and virtue, by which have been given to us ***exceedingly great and precious promises, that through these you may be partakers of the divine nature,*** having escaped the corruption that is in the world through lust. **2 PETER 1:2-4**

Grace and peace is multiplied (2 Peter 1:2-4) as we grow in the ***revelation*** of all He provided by His Finished Work. In the continual renewing of our mind, looking through the mind of Christ, we partake of the divine nature.

ABSORBING DEEPER

1/ What was *the great exchange* in the Crown of Thorns?

_____

_____

_____

2/ What do thorns represent?

_____

3/ What does the ground represent?

_____

4/ What is the seed?

_____

5/ Explain what happens when the Word is planted deep in our hearts. What are the results in our life?

_____

_____

_____

_____

6/ Explain what happens when the Word falls among the thorns. What are results in our life?

_____

_____

_____

_____

_____

REFLECT AND DISCUSS

7/ How is worry void of understanding of the Finished Work? Explain why this carnal thinking is rooted in self-reliance. Can you see evidence in your own life? HINT: We all do.

_____

_____

_____

_____

_____

8/ Give some examples of how the Word planted deep in your heart produced a supernatural result?

_____

_____

_____

_____

9/ What does it mean to know all things and have the mind of Christ?

_____

_____

_____

_____

10/How can we learn to live from this relationship all the time?

_____

_____

_____

_____

C. THE CROSS

THE SENTENCE PAID FOR OUR SPIRIT

⬤ Jesus carried that Cross up the mountain, after barely surviving the Whipping Post that left His body beyond recognition. After having the Crown of Thorns beaten into his skull with the full force of clubs and the sting of spit and mockery, *He willingly carrie♦ it.*

With legions of angels ready and able, at the tiniest word of His command, to mete retribution and relieve Him from this relentless torture, why did He go on?

Jesus Christ, the Anointed One, the second person of the Godhead, *the Word who is God,* who was in the beginning with God, and without Him nothing was made—He put on flesh *for this very moment* (John 1:1-5). He went all the way up that hill willingly, *even with joy* (Hebrews 12-2)! Why?

In the beginning was the Word, and the Word was with God, and the Word was God. He was in the beginning with God. All things were made through Him, and without Him nothing was made that was made. *In Him was life, and the life was the light of men.* And the light shines in the darkness, and the darkness did not comprehend it. JOHN 1:1-5

looking unto Jesus, the author and finisher of our faith, *who for the joy that was set before Him endured the cross,* despising the shame, and has sat down at the right hand of the throne of God. HEBREWS 12:2

Jesus bore the Cross, and the whole torturous sentence, to love us with every ounce of Himself, unconditionally, *whether we accepte♦ Him or not!*

But God, who is rich in mercy, *because of His great love with which He loved us*, even when we were dead in trespasses, made us alive together with Christ (by grace you have been saved), and raised us up together, and made us sit together in the heavenly places in Christ Jesus, that in the ages to come He might show the exceeding riches of His grace in His kindness toward us in Christ Jesus. For by grace you have been saved through faith, and that not of yourselves; it is the gift of God, not of works, lest anyone should boast. EPHESIANS 2:4-9

Jesus bore our sin **in exchange** for His righteousness. Every drop of his blood poured out, every agonizing minute, every breath—He joyfully gave to us so *we* could have forgiveness of sins; so *we* could have liberty from every oppression; so *we* could be restored to personal, intimate relationship with Him; so *we* could be honored and seated in Christ at His right hand for all eternity; so *we* could experience in the ages to come the exceeding riches of His grace and kindness toward us (Ephesians 2:4-9).

> Beloved, let us love one another, for love is of God; and everyone who loves is born of God and knows God. He who does not love does not know God, **for God is love**. In this the love of God was manifested toward us, **that God has sent His only begotten Son into the world, that we might live through Him.** In this is love, **not that we loved God, but that He loved us** and sent His Son to be the propitiation for our sins. Beloved, if God so loved us, we also ought to love one another. **1 JOHN 4:7-11**

In these harrowing hours *He loved us with all the love that the God of heaven and earth is—for He is love* (1 John 4:7-11).

He poured out His love willingly, with the perfect obedience that would triumph over every evil *for all eternity*—for each and every one of us, individually, personally.

Why? In one solitary word—*love*.

THE PASSOVER LAMB

The passover lamb is the shadow, and Jesus, the perfect *lamb of God[1] who took away the sins of the world,* is the substance (John 1:29).

> The next day John saw Jesus coming toward him, and said, "Behold! *The Lamb of God[1] who takes away the sin of the world!* **JOHN 1:29**

> Then the Lord said to Moses, "Go in to Pharaoh and tell him, 'Thus says the Lord God of the Hebrews: *"Let My people go*, that they may serve Me. **EXODUS 9:1**

When Moses repeatedly appeared before Pharaoh to demand *"let my people go,"* the great plagues were unleashed on Egypt (Exodus 9:1). Ravished by nine out of the ten, this was Pharaoh's last chance to comply. The final plague was going to be the worst—the death of the firstborn male.

> Speak to all the congregation of Israel, saying: 'On the tenth of this month every man shall take for himself a lamb, according to the house of his father, a lamb for a household. **EXODUS 12:3**
>
> *Your lamb shall be without blemish,*[1] ... Then the whole assembly of the congregation of Israel shall *kill it at twilight*. And they shall *take some of the blood*[2] *and put it on the two doorposts and on the lintel of the houses* where they eat it. **EXODUS 12:5-7**
>
> 'For I will pass through the land of Egypt on that night, and will strike all *the firstborn*[3] in the land of Egypt, ...both man and beast; and against all the gods of Egypt I will *execute judgment:*[4] I am the Lord. *Now the blood*[2] *shall be a sign for you on the houses where you are. And when I see the blood, I will pass over*[5] *you;* ... and the plague shall not be on you to destroy you when I strike the land of Egypt. 'So this day shall be to you a memorial; and you shall keep it as a feast to the Lord throughout your generations. You shall keep it as a feast by an everlasting ordinance. **EXODUS 12:12-14**

The instructions of the first passover were given to Moses for all the children of Israel. The *lamb without blemish*[1] was to be killed at twilight. The *blood*[2] *of the lamb*[1] *brushed on the doorposts and lintel* would save the *firstborn male*[3] of that household. The death angel, the one that brings *judgment,*[4] *passed over*[5] at the sign of the *blood*[2] sacrifice (Exodus 12:3, 5-7, 12-14).

THE SHADOWS AND TYPES

Egypt represents all of fallen mankind, who inherit the corruption of sin which came from Adam (Romans 5:12).

The *firstborn male*[3] is the heir and his *inheritance*[4] is death—the sentence for the penalty of sin.

The *lamb*[1] represents Jesus, His *blood*[2] shed for our guilt. When *His blood*[2] *is on the doorposts of our heart,* the death angel *passes over*[5] us and eternally frees us from the *judgment*[4] of sin (Hebrews 9:22).

> Therefore, just as through one man sin entered the world, and death through sin, and thus death spread to all men, because all sinned— **ROMANS 5:12**
>
> Indeed, under the law almost everything is purified with *blood,*[2] and without the shedding of *blood*[2] there is no forgiveness of sins. **HEBREWS 9:22 ESV**

OUR LAMB IS WITHOUT BLEMISH

The sacrificial *lamb*[1] had to be perfect. When a person brought their offering to the priest, the *lamb*[1] was examined, never the person.

👥 Thanks to God, this picture not only applies to us, but *it is the shadow and type of us.* We are never examined to see if we are perfect and blameless. We would never pass inspection.

> knowing that you were not redeemed with corruptible things, like silver or gold, from your aimless conduct received by tradition from your fathers, but with *the precious blood*[2] *of Christ, as of a lamb*[1] *without blemish and without spot.* **1 PETER 1:18-19**
>
> For He made Him who knew no sin to be sin for us, that we might become the righteousness of God in Him. **2 CORINTHIANS 5:21**
>
> And you know that He was manifested to take away our sins, and in Him there is no sin. **1 JOHN 3:5**
>
> "Who committed no sin, nor was deceit found in His mouth"; **1 PETER 2:22**
>
> For we do not have a High Priest who cannot sympathize with our weaknesses, but was in all points tempted as we are, yet without sin. **HEBREWS 4:15**

As we come before God with our perfect *lamb,*[1] Jesus has been examined in our place, and He was found *without spot or wrinkle* (1 Peter 1:18-19, 2 Corinthians 5:21, 1 John 3:5, 1 Peter 2:22, Hebrews 4:15).

SHADOW AND SUBSTANCE TOGETHER

👥 Jesus was sacrificed *at the very same hour the high priest was performing the passover in the temple.* While he was carrying out the sacrifice to cover the sins of Israel for the next year, the *Lamb of God*[1] was being sacrificed to cover *all the sins of all mankind for all eternity.*

💧 Just imagine the chief priests and elders who had planned and carried out his death. They had no concept of these shadows and types. Their timing couldn't be more perfect. Clearly timed by God, *the shadow and the substance were sacrificed at the very same time!*

THE VEIL TORN

The Holy of Holies, where the presence of God abided, was separated from the rest of the temple by the veil, a huge curtain made of thick layers of different materials. Only the high priest could enter behind the veil and only once a year to offer the passover sacrifice, by which, the children of Israel received salvation for a year.

👤 This shadow and type of the veil represents the separation we were born into, Adam having lost our Spirit-to-spirit relationship with God at the fall (Chapter 2).

When Jesus cried out, "My God, why have you forsaken me" this was the horrifying moment when He who was without sin became sin on our behalf (Matthew 27:45-46, 2 Corinthians 5:21).

The moment Jesus yielded His spirit and took his last breath, the sky was dark, the earth shook, and *the veil in the temple was torn in two* (Matthew 27:50-51).

> Now from the sixth hour until the ninth hour there was darkness over all the land. And about the ninth hour Jesus cried out with a loud voice, saying, "Eli, Eli, lama sabachthani?" that is, "My God, My God, why have You forsaken Me?" **MATTHEW 27:45-46**
>
> For He made Him who knew no sin to be sin for us, that we might become the righteousness of God in Him. **2 CORINTHIANS 5:21**
>
> And Jesus cried out again with a loud voice, and yielded up His spirit. Then, behold, *the veil of the temple was torn in two from top to bottom;* and the earth quaked, and the rocks were split, **MATTHEW 27:50-51**

No earthly phenomenon could have done it. Precisely, it was torn *from top to bottom, from heaven to earth.* 👤 Clearly it was God who tore the veil, *signifying the separation between God and man was over.* Through receiving Christ (Chapter 13), our *Lamb*[1] without blemish, we are restored to perfect Spirit-to-spirit relationship.

He is our High Priest now and the mediator of the New Covenant. He executed the Covenant once and for all. Now, He forever lives to make

> Also there were many priests, because they were prevented by death from continuing. *But He, because He continues forever, has an unchangeable priesthood.* Therefore He is also able to save to the uttermost those who come to God through Him, since *He always lives to make intercession* for them. HEBREWS 7:23-25

> Therefore, brethren, *having boldness to enter the Holiest by the blood of Jesus, by a new and living way which He consecrated for us, through the veil,* that is, His flesh, and having a High Priest over the house of God, let us draw near with a true heart in full assurance of faith, *having our hearts sprinkled from an evil conscience* and our bodies washed with pure water. HEBREWS 10:19-22

intercession for us because unlike all the high priests of the Old Covenant, He will never die (Hebrews 7:23-25).

🜄 We can enter into God's presence and draw near with boldness. We *have obtained mercy and shall find grace to help in every time of need* all because of His blood on the doorposts and lintel of our heart (Hebrews 10:19-22, 4:16).

> Let us therefore come boldly to the throne of grace, that we may *obtain mercy and find grace to help in time of need.* HEBREWS 4:16

> And when they had come to the place called Calvary, there they crucified Him LUKE 23:33

> And He, bearing His cross, went out to a place called the Place of a Skull, which is called in Hebrew, Golgotha, JOHN 19:17

JESUS CRUCIFIED ON GOLGOTHA

Jesus was crucified on a mountain called Calvary (Luke 23:33). The Hebrew translation is Golgotha, which means the place of a skull (John 19:17).

There is a fascinating relationship between Golgotha and one of the most famous stories in the Old Testament—David and Goliath.

Goliath of Gath, or Gola Gatha. How similar is his name to Golgotha? This could hardly be a coincidence. But before we analyze the connection, let's go back to the pronouncement of the curse, when God was addressing the serpent for what he had done to deceive Adam and Eve.

The Seed of the woman (Jesus) will bruise, or crush, the serpents head, and he, the serpent, would bruise His heel (Genesis 3:15).

👤 Keeping this in mind, let's observe some shadows and types in the story of David and Goliath:

> And I will put enmity between you and the woman, and between your seed and her Seed; He shall bruise your head, and you shall bruise His heel."
> **GENESIS 3:15**

David was God's man, a man after God's own heart, and knew Him personally. He experienced God's deliverance from the lion and the bear. He was too young to be a soldier in the army of Israel, yet he was the only one who understood the covenant God had made with them. While they were shaking in their armor, listening to Goliath's words of fear, David fearlessly declared, "this uncircumcised Philistine will be like one of them [bear/lion], *seeing he has defied the armies of the living God"* (1 Samuel 17:36).

> Your servant has killed both lion and bear; and *this uncircumcised Philistine will be like one of them, seeing he has defied the armies of the living God."*
> **1 SAMUEL 17:36**

Understanding *circumcision represents covenant with God,* Goliath was the champion, the representative of the armies of the *uncircumcised* (no covenant). Essentially, he was the representative of the devil, and a great picture for us to meditate on.

His physical appearance was formidable. He cursed Israel, representing the curse of the law. This is exactly what the devil does today in our mind using the natural circumstances that challenge us daily. *He uses fear and focuses on getting us to doubt the Word of God* (Chapters 1 and 2). If we take fear's bait, we are looking at our own ability (or inability). *Self-focused, we are back under the curse of the law* and unable to access His *grace by faith* (Chapters 4 and 7, Hebrews 4:16 p108).

Merely a youth of 17, David knew this giant that towered and raged had no power over a servant of the Most High. *He was covered, protected and backed by the Living God.* He knew it, because he had revelation understanding through relationship with God.

> Then David said to the Philistine, "You come to me with a sword, with a spear, and with a javelin. *But I come to you in the name of the LORD of hosts, the God of the armies of Israel, whom you have defied.* This day the LORD will deliver you into my hand, and I will strike you *and take your head from you*... 1 SAMUEL 17:45-46

David took his *staff,*[6] which represents the *Word,*[6] and *five smooth stones. Five*[7] is the number of *grace*[7] and the *stones*[8] represent *the rock of revelation*[8] *the church is built upon* (p122).

With the automatic faith that arises from *revelation*[8] understanding, exactly as he boldly declared in 1 Samuel 17:45-46, David took Goliath's head off—the head of the serpent (Genesis 3:15)!

In other words, *by having the revelation*[8] *of grace*[7] *through the Messiah,* by believing and receiving, David took the head off the enemy. Now remember, David is a shadow and type and Christ is the substance.

According to 1 Samuel 17:54, David carried his head all the way back to Jerusalem to prove his victory and claim the spoils. Undoubtedly, David buried Goliath's skull on the highest hill and that mountain became known as Golgotha, the place of a skull.

💧 *Jesus was crucified with the head of the enemy literally under His feet* (Genesis 3:15). Spiritually, through Jesus being *bruised for our iniquity* (Isaiah 53:5), He put his heel upon the neck of the devil, and the serpent was crushed, once and for all *under His feet!*

> And David took the head of the Philistine and brought it to Jerusalem... 1 SAMUEL 17:54
>
> But He was wounded for our transgressions, *He was bruised for our iniquities;* the chastisement for our peace was upon Him, and by His stripes we are healed. ISAIAH 53:5

All these shadows and types are the picture of who we are today in Christ. By the Finished Work, God took the head off the enemy once and for all.

THE DEVIL IS UNDER OUR FEET

Jesus sits at the right hand of God the Father and the devil is under His feet (Psalm 110:1). Now we've been raised up *together* and *seated together* in Him, the devil is under our feet (Ephesians 2:6).

> The Lord says to my Lord: "Sit at my right hand, until I make your enemies your footstool." **PSALM 110:1**
>
> and *raised us up together, and made us sit together* in the heavenly places in Christ Jesus, **EPHESIANS 2:6**
>
> Behold, I have given you authority to tread on serpents and scorpions, and over all the power of the enemy, and nothing shall hurt you. **LUKE 10:19**

Luke 10:19 is a clear directive from Jesus' mouth to us—we have been given power and delegated authority *over all the power of the enemy.* Meditating on scriptures like these in fellowship with the Holy Spirit will cause revelation faith to arise in us. Just like David, *we'll run towards the enemy,* automatically knowing that *we are backed by the Living God.*

OUR FEET SHOD WITH THE GOSPEL

Contrary to popular teaching on Ephesians 6:15, having our feet shod with the gospel is not an evangelistic reference about sharing the gospel.

> and having shod your feet with the *preparation*[9] of the gospel of peace; **EPHESIANS 6:15**

Sharing our faith is definitely what we have been called to do, but this whole passage on the armor of God is about how we withstand the attacks of the enemy in the spiritual warfare of the mind.

When our feet are shod with the *gospel of peace*, it means we are standing firmly in the truth of having been *restored to peace with God.* No matter the circumstance, we know we are forgiven, blessed, protected, favored and backed by the Living God. Our shoes *prepare*[9] us to walk *ready*[9] for anything the enemy tries to throw at us. *We never cower in fear at the taunt of the giant.*

His Word, the revelation of Jesus, is the lamp that shows us *exactly where we stand in Christ* in restored relationship (Psalm 119:105). Submitting to His leadership, we stand immovable on grace ground.

> Your word is a lamp to my feet and a light to my path. **PSALM 119:105**

THE POWER IS IN THE BLOOD

Paying the price of death with His own blood He obtained our eternal redemption once and for all. Absolutely everything we couldn't do under the Old Covenant, He did for us in the New (Hebrews 9:12-15).

> Not with the blood of goats and calves, *but with His own blood He entered the Most Holy Place once for all, having obtained eternal redemption.* For if the blood of bulls and goats and the ashes of a heifer, sprinkling the unclean, sanctifies for the purifying of the flesh, how much more shall the blood of Christ, who through the eternal Spirit offered Himself without spot to God, *cleanse your conscience from dead works to serve the living God?* And for this reason He is the Mediator of the new covenant, by means of death, for the redemption of the transgressions under the first covenant, *that those who are called may receive the promise of the eternal inheritance.* **HEBREWS 9:12-15**

Everything we are in the New Covenant is because of the precious blood of Christ:

Forgiveness of sins is in the blood.
Life is in the blood.
Power is in the blood.

As we take Communion often, we take care to distinguish *the bread from the wine, the body from the blood* (p86). But the more we meditate on what was won by His blood, the more liberty and power we will see evident in our lives (Matthew 26:26-28). Through understanding the blood, we'll appropriate His *life more abundantly.* (John 10:10).

> And as they were eating, Jesus took bread, blessed and broke it, and gave it to the disciples and said, "Take, eat; this is My body." Then He took the cup, and gave thanks, and gave it to them, saying, "Drink from it, all of you. *For this is My blood of the new covenant, which is shed for many for the remission of sins.* **MATTHEW 26:26-28**

> ... I have come that they may have life, and that they may have it more abundantly. **JOHN 10:10**

SUMMARIZING THE SENTENCE THROUGH ISAIAH 53:5

But He was wounded for our transgressions, He was bruised for our iniquities; the chastisement for our peace was upon Him, and by His stripes we are healed. **ISAIAH 53:5**

This one verse encapsulates such depth of understanding of the sentence that Jesus paid for us, and describes how each part covered our 3-part being. Let's look at each phrase:

But He was **wounded** for our **transgressions**,

Wounds break the skin and represent the outer man, the **flesh**. Transgressions are the outward acts of rebellion—sins.

He was **bruised** for our **iniquities**;

Bruises are under the skin and represent the **spirit**. Iniquities happen in the heart where sin is conceived. The iniquity of the heart causes the outward transgression.

the **chastisement for our peace** was upon Him,

The chastisement is the blood shed so we can have peace with God. When there's no peace with God, there's torment of the mind from the condemnation of sin. **Soul.**

and **by His stripes we are healed**

Healing of the **body.**

IT IS FINISHED

On the Cross when Jesus cried out "It is finished," He declared *the sentence for the condemnation that was upon all of mankind had been carried out* (John 19:30). The price of death that each and every one of us owed was paid and the righteous requirement of the law was fulfilled (Romans 8:3-4).

> So when Jesus had received the sour wine, He said, **"It is finished!"** And bowing His head, He gave up His spirit. **JOHN 19:30**
>
> For what the law could not do in that it was weak through the flesh, **God did by sending His own Son** in the likeness of sinful flesh, on account of sin: He condemned sin in the flesh, **that the righteous requirement of the law might be fulfilled** in us who do not walk according to the flesh but according to the Spirit. **ROMANS 8:3-4**

But there was more to do in the Finished Work. What happened between the grave and the Throne? There were important last steps that Jesus walked out to take hold of the final victory.

ABSORBING DEEPER

1/ What was *the great exchange* in the Cross?

_____

2/ Why did Jesus willingly, even joyfully, go all the way to the Cross?

_____

_____

_____

3/ What was the result of Jesus pouring out His love on the Cross?

_____

_____

4/ What is the Passover lamb a shadow and type of?

_____

_____

5/ What does Egypt represent?

_____

6/ Who is the heir and what is his inheritance?

_____

_____

7/ Why was the blood of the lamb brushed on the doorposts and the lintel of the door? What does it represent?

_____

_____

_____

_____

8/ When a person brought their sacrificial lamb to the temple, what did the priest do? How does this relate to us today? What is the substance of this shadow?

_____

_____

_____

9/ Explain how the shadow and substance were sacrificed at the same time at Jesus' crucification.

_____

_____

_____

10/ What was the purpose of the veil in the temple and what did it represent?

_____

_____

_____

11/ Why was the veil in the temple torn in two, and what did it represent? Who tore it and how do we know this?

_____

_____

_____

_____

12/ What is the significance of Jesus being crucified on Golgotha? Use Genesis 3:15 to explain.

_____

_____

_____

REFLECT AND DISCUSS

13/How is Goliath a picture of how the enemy comes against us day-to-day? Can you see some examples of his tactics in your life?

_____

_____

_____

_____

_____

14/If David took up his staff and five smooth stones to overcome the enemy, how do we?

_____

_____

_____

_____

_____

15/By the Finished Work, God took the head off the enemy once and for all. How does this change how you view your life and present circumstances? What are the obvious and automatic actions and words arising in you as a result of this revelation?

_____

_____

_____

_____

_____

16/Have you uncovered some areas the enemy had been taunting you without you even knowing it? How have you been blinded to your power and authority in Christ?

_____

_____

_____

_____

17/How can David's fearless attitude through personally knowing the Lord increase in you? HINT: You can't make it happen in your own strength.

_____

_____

_____

_____

18/What does Ephesians 6:15 mean and how does it apply to you?

_____

_____

_____

_____

19/How do you understand Psalm 119:105 differently than before?

_____

_____

_____

_____

20/Meditating on the power of Jesus' blood, what are some practical ways it applies to your life? Take Communion, discerning the blood and wine from the body and bread. Meditate on all these things to receive continual revelation.

_____

_____

_____

_____

_____

_____

21/Using Isaiah 53:5, summarize the three parts of the sentence that cover our three-part being.

_____

_____

_____

_____

_____

_____

_____

22/What is the significance of the sentence being finished?

_____

_____

_____

_____

_____

_____

PART FOUR

THE VICTORY

> So when this corruptible has put on incorruption, and this mortal has put on immortality, then shall be brought to pass the saying that is written: *"Death is swallowed up in victory." "O Death, where is your sting? O Hades, where is your victory?" The sting of death is sin, and the strength of sin is the law. But thanks be to God, who gives us the victory through our Lord Jesus Christ.* 1 CORINTHIANS 15:54-57

Thanks be to God, death is defeated *right now.* ● Even though the final victory is when death is *completely swallowed up* and we receive our resurrected flesh, we have been freed from death, freed from the law which is the strength of sin, and we have the victory right now through our Lord Jesus Christ (1 Corinthians 15:54-57).

There are three parts to the Victory: The keys of the Kingdom, the Mercy Seat and the Throne.

A. THE KEYS OF THE KINGDOM

When Jesus went into the grave, He went to hell and took back the keys—plural.

The keys of Hades (hell) and death are what had imprisoned us (Revelation 1:18). Hell is the place, and death is the sentence.

> I am He who lives, and was dead, and behold, I am alive forevermore... And I have *the keys of Hades and of Death.* REVELATION 1:18

But now, we have been loosed from condemnation unto death, the sentence that God assigned for sin. Jesus freed us from eternal condemnation and won back our dominion and authority over the earth. Even though the devil is still the ruler of this corrupted, fallen earth, in Christ, we are not subject *under* his rule. The devil is *under our feet,* right now (p111).

We were *locked out* of relationship with God. But when Jesus got the keys, He *bound* the separation of death and *loosed* us into the New Creation reality.

PETER'S REVELATION OF JESUS AS THE CHRIST

In Matthew 16:15-17, when Jesus asked Peter "Who do you say that I am," Peter got the *revelation*[1] from heaven—Jesus is the Christ, the Messiah, the One that all of Israel had been waiting for.

He said to them, *"But who do you say that I am?"* Simon Peter answered and said, *"You are the Christ, the Son of the living God."* Jesus answered and said to him, "Blessed are you, Simon Bar-Jonah, for flesh and blood has not *revealed*[1] this to you, but My Father who is in heaven. And I also say to you that you are Peter, and *on this rock I will build My church,* and the gates of Hades shall not prevail against it. 18 And I will give you the keys of the kingdom of heaven, and whatever you bind on earth will be bound in heaven, and whatever you loose on earth will be loosed in heaven." MATTHEW 16:15-19

For as Jonah was three days and three nights in the belly of the great fish, so will the Son of Man be three days and three nights in the heart of the earth. MATTHEW 12:40

In Jesus' response, He said "... Simon Bar Jonah..." which means Simon, son of Jonah. Whether Peter's immediate father was named Jonah, or he was a descendant of the original prophet, Jonah, or both, the reference is significant.

Jonah was a shadow and type of Jesus. He was a prophet who God called to *prophesy* repentance to Nineveh. Instead of obeying, he ended up being swallowed by a whale (read Jonah 1-4). In Matthew 12:40, the reference to him

121

spending three days in the belly of the whale is likened to Jesus being three days in the grave.

Now back to the *revelation*[1] of Peter. As we look at the rest of the passage (Matthew 16:18-19), by referencing Jonah, we can conclude He was essentially communicating something along these lines:

> While I'm gone for three days in the grave, I'll be getting the keys of the kingdom for you. By these keys your authority is restored and you'll have the ability to **bind and loose** here on earth, and heaven (the spirit realm) has to obey.

THE ROCK OF REVELATION

Now when Jonah finally submitted to being obedient to God's instruction, he returned and prophesied to Nineveh by *revelation*[1] from the Lord and the whole city got *saved*.[2]

The significant conclusion is that *salvation*[2] is a result of *revelation.*[1] Not just eternal *salvation,*[2] but everyday deliverance, protection and provision kind of *salvation.*[2]

Revelation[1] *is the rock Jesus is building His church upon* (Matthew 16:18-19). The gates of hell have no power to hold us anymore. But also, we appropriate *salvation*[2] in our everyday life by receiving *revelation*[1] through our restored Spirit-to-spirit relationship.

It's important to connect here that *revelation*[1] comes from relationship through the Holy Spirit. Power is released when we speak and do *only what our Father says* (John 5:19). This is how Jesus operated in His supernatural ministry here on earth. He could do nothing of Himself.

> **4982 SÓZÓ:**[2] (sode'-zo) to save, heal, preserve, rescue. † From sōs, safe, rescued. Deliver out of danger and into safety; used principally of God *rescuing believers from the penalty and power of sin and into His provisions (safety).* The root of **4990 SŌTÉR** Savior, **4991 SŌTĒRĺA** salvation and **4992 SŌTÉRION** what is saved, or rescued from destruction and brought into divine safety.

Always secure by being based on fellowship in the Word of God, this is the same way the church is continually being built upon the rock of **revelation[1] relationship**.

It takes purposeful submission to learn and grow in our ability to clearly perceive God's instruction. We weren't born into relationship like Adam was, so developing our spiritual senses takes focused effort. It's extremely common for believers to be confused and

> Then Jesus answered and said to them, "Most assuredly, I say to you, **the Son can do nothing of Himself, but what He sees the Father do**; for whatever He does, the Son also does in like manner. **JOHN 5:19**

unsure if they have "heard" correctly. It's easy for us to be listening to our own reasoning, or even another spirit. Many are deceived and don't even know it. But we should receive no condemnation about this—born separated, we all have to learn to correctly and **biblically** discern the leading of the Lord.

Speak It:® 30 Days of Saturation in the Spirit-Empowere▪ Life is an in-depth study into our restored relationship. Through saturating our understanding through the Word we will appropriate deeper and deeper **revelation[1]** in **relationship**.

THE KEYS UNLOCK OUR INHERITANCE

When we stand on what is done in heaven, we have eternal access to it now here on earth. When we **bind and loose,** heaven will comply based on what Jesus has already supplied. Continual **revelation[1]** of the Finished Work unlocks what we didn't know was ours:

> And my God shall supply all your need according to his riches in glory by Christ Jesus. **PHILIPPIANS 4:19**

Looking in the natural, we think we're poor when our bank account is low;

But in Christ, we are rich. He supplies our every need according to His riches in glory (Philippians 4:19).

Looking in the natural, when we experience a symptom in our body, we think we are sick;

But in Christ, by His stripes we are the healed of the Lord. There is no cause for the curse to come upon our body and no weapon formed against us shall prosper (Proverbs 26:2, 1 Peter 2:24, Isaiah 54:17).

Looking in the natural, we think we are in bondage when addictive behavior tries to take hold;

But in Christ, we stand steadfast in the liberty by which Christ has set us free (Galatians 5:1). We submit to God, resist the devil and he flees from us (James 4:7).

Looking in the natural, we tend to think adverse circumstances mean we should be fearful;

But in Christ, He causes our feet to walk like hinds feet over every mountainous trial (Psalm 18:33). We cast our cares onto Him and He cares for us (1 Peter 5:7).

> Like a flitting sparrow, like a flying swallow, so a curse without cause shall not alight. **PROVERBS 26:2**
>
> ... by whose stripes *you were healed*. **1 PETER 2:24**
>
> No weapon formed against you shall prosper... **ISAIAH 54:17**
>
> Stand fast therefore in the liberty by which Christ has made us free, and do not be entangled again with a yoke of bondage. **GALATIANS 5:1**
>
> Therefore submit to God. Resist the devil and he will flee from you. **JAMES 4:7**
>
> He makes my feet like the feet of deer, and sets me on my high places. **PSALM 18:33**
>
> casting all your care upon Him, for He cares for you. **1 PETER 5:7**
>
> But we all, with unveiled face, *beholding as in a mirror the glory of the Lord,* are being transformed into the same image *from glory to glory,*[3] just as by the Spirit of the Lord. **2 CORINTHIANS 3:18**

REVELATION *IS* THE KEY(S)

🜄 *It's in beholding Him* that we are changed—it's the *revelation*[1] of His Finished Work that changes us and *looses us* into our inheritance. As we gaze into the mirror of His face, *we see ourselves and everything He won for us,* and we are transformed (2 Corinthians 3:18).

Through *revelation*[1] faith arises automatically and we act differently—we act according to faith. It's easy to **set our minds on things above** (Colossians 3:2). We've moved *from the glory of the law and the Old Covenant to the glory of the New!*[3]

Set your mind on things above, not on things on the earth.
COLOSSIANS 3:2

This continual, growing *revelation* of Jesus' Finished Work *is the same key* that locks out condemnation, fear, sickness, shame, and lack—every argument the devil uses to deceive us loses its power. As opposed to putting faith in the devil (Chapters 1 and 2), putting more faith in the Word of God is our new effortless reality.

ABSORBING DEEPER

1/ What is the difference between the final victory and the victory we have right now?

_____

_____

2/ What is the first thing Jesus did after His death on the Cross?

_____

_____

3/ When Jesus got the keys, He **bound** _____

and **loosed** us into _____

4/ If the devil is the ruler over the corrupted world, how do we have the victory right now? See p111 and 120.

_____

_____

5/ Explain how Peter's revelation in Matthew 16:15-19 is related to the keys of the kingdom?

_____

_____

6/ What is the rock that the church is built upon?

_____

7/ How are revelation and salvation connected?

_____

_____

_____

8/ What are some things included in salvation here and now?

_____

_____

_____

9/ What is the key(s) that unlocks our inheritance? Describe how to use the keys and how it causes us to act differently.

_____

_____

_____

_____

_____

_____

REFLECT AND DISCUSS

10/ Write down some provisions that Jesus supplied through the Finished Work that you have not been fully accessing. For example, how "saved" are your finances? How "saved" is your physical body? How "saved" are your relationships? Whether your salvation in these areas is apparent or not, you have access to way more than you might think. How can you access salvation and unlock your eternal inheritance now? Find some scriptures that support these things and make them your meditation and confession until revelation opens the doors that previously seemed to be locked.

_____

_____

_____

_____

_____

_____

_____

_____

_____

_____

_____

_____

11/Do you see how there is no end to receiving revelation of the Finished Work of Christ? Write down some things you thought were impossible until now.

_____

_____

_____

_____

_____

12/How do you think differently about salvation now?

_____

_____

_____

_____

_____

B. THE MERCY SEAT

The mercy seat is the lid of the ark of the covenant. Essentially it's a coffin that carried *all the symbols of man's rebellion*, all of which have been *put to death under the blood of Christ.*

Inside were the two tablets of stone with the Ten Commandments written on them, symbolizing *man's rebellion against God's laws*; a golden pot of manna, symbolizing *man's rejection of God's provision*; Aaron's rod that budded, symbolizing *man's rebellion against God's authority* (Hebrews 9:4-5).

Jesus went to hell and got the keys of Hades and death, but death couldn't hold Him there. He paid the price for all mankind and because He was blameless, *death had no hold on Him* and He was resurrected by the power of the Holy Spirit (Acts 2:24).

which had the golden censer and the ark of the covenant overlaid on all sides with gold, in which were the golden pot that had the manna, Aaron's rod that budded, and the tablets of the covenant; and above it were the cherubim of glory overshadowing the mercy seat... HEBREWS 9:4-5

whom God raised up, having loosed the pains of death, because *it was not possible that He should be held by it.* ACTS 2:24

He shall take some of the blood of the bull and sprinkle it with his finger *on the mercy seat* LEVITICUS 16:14

But Christ came as High Priest of the good things to come, with the greater and more perfect tabernacle not made with hands, that is, not of this creation. Not with the blood of goats and calves, *but with His own blood He entered the Most Holy Place once for all,* having obtained eternal redemption. For if the blood of bulls and goats and the ashes of a heifer, sprinkling the unclean, sanctifies for the purifying of the flesh, how much more shall the blood of Christ, who through the eternal Spirit offered Himself without spot to God, cleanse your conscience from dead works to serve the living God? And for this reason He is the Mediator of the new covenant, by means of death, for the redemption of the transgressions under the first covenant, that those who are called may receive the promise of the eternal inheritance. HEBREWS 9:11-15

👤 In the shadow and type, the blood of a bull was sprinkled on the mercy seat (Leviticus 16:14). After His resurrection, Jesus, being the substance, *sprinkled His blood on the mercy seat in heaven.*

As depicted in the cover of this book, two cherubim are gazing down on the mercy seat. These cherubim represent the same angels that were left guarding the tree of life at the entrance of the Garden of Eden (Chapter 2). When Jesus sprinkled His blood He was showing them *proof that the blood payment for the sin of all mankind had been paid.* Jesus was essentially declaring to them, "you can give them (us) access to the tree of life now. The curse has been removed and eternal life is granted."

All the rebellion of mankind is under the blood, we have received the mercy of God, and eternal justification is now the foundation of our relationship.

THE FLAMING SWORD

Back in Genesis, when the cherubim were set in place guarding the tree of life, they were given a flaming sword (Genesis 3:22-24).

👤 The sword represents the Word, which is Jesus and His Finished Work.

The fire represents the baptism by fire. This is a rich and detailed topic to study (Chapter 6 of *Speak It:® 30 Days of Saturation in the Spirit-Empowere• Life*). But in brief, the baptism by fire is a sanctifying and purifying process that separates our spirit man from the flesh. *Revelation[1]* in relationship with the Holy Spirit, is the actual sanctifying and purifying agent.

> ... And now, lest he put out his hand and take also of the tree of life, and eat, and live forever" — therefore the Lord God sent him out of the garden of Eden to till the ground from which he was taken. So He drove out the man; and He placed cherubim at the east of the garden of Eden, and *a flaming sword* which turned every way, to guard the way to the tree of life. **GENESIS 3:22-24**

So putting the two together, the flaming sword is a picture of the *revelation[1]* of the Finished Work.

🩸 Now the flaming sword was turning every way to guard the tree of life. So to get to the tree of life, you have to go through the flaming sword—**you have to get revelation[1] about the Finished Work and claim salvation by the blood of Christ** (Chapter 13) **to get to the tree of life!**

JESUS' BLOOD IS GOD'S MERCY

The very next thing recorded after the fall of man was the first murder. In Genesis 4, Cain killed his brother, Abel.

> By faith **Abel offered to God a more excellent sacrifice than Cain**, through which he obtained witness that he was righteous, God testifying of his gifts; and through it he being dead still speaks. **HEBREWS 11:4**

> And He said, "What have you done? The voice of **your brother's blood cries out to Me** from the ground. **GENESIS 4:10**

👤 Cain was jealous because Abel's offering to God (a blood sacrifice) was accepted, while his own offering from the work of his hands, was rejected (Hebrews 11:4).

This is such a significant shadow and type from so early in scripture. ❶ This first mention of offerings and sacrifices proves the work of the hands is rejected in God's eyes. Nothing but a blood sacrifice is acceptable.

Genesis 4:10 declares that Abel's **blood cried out** with a voice of condemnation. This represents the requirement of the law that demands an eye for an eye, a tooth for a tooth (Exodus 21:23-24). It shouts that we're going to get what we deserve—which is death.

> But if any harm follows, then you shall give life for life, eye for eye, tooth for tooth, hand for hand, foot for foot, **EXODUS 21:23-24**

🩸 But Jesus' blood sprinkled is God's mercy poured out for us. The mercy seat is the lid on the coffin of all of man's rebellion. The voice of

> to Jesus the Mediator of the new covenant, and to **the blood of sprinkling that speaks better things than that of Abel.**
> **HEBREWS 12:24**
>
> But if we walk in the light as He is in the light, we have fellowship with one another, and the blood of Jesus Christ His Son **cleanses**[1] us from all sin. **1 JOHN 1:7**

condemnation that was crying out has been silenced and put to death by the blood of Jesus (Hebrews 12:24).

Now **His blood**[3] is **constantly**[2] **speaking** mercy and grace,

KEY GREEK WORD

2511 KATHARIZÓ:[1] (kath-ar-id'-zo) to cleanse. ⚷ Present tense —**continuous action in progress**[2] or a state of persistence. Active voice—the subject, **Jesus' blood,**[3] is performing the action.

and **continually**[2] **cleansing**[1] us from sin (1 John 1:7). It cries out righteousness and justification as a witness of our **eternal justification** to all of heaven.

ABSORBING DEEPER

1/ Jesus went to hell and got the keys. What happened next and Who did it?

_____

_____

2/ Why was death unable to hold Him?

_____

_____

3/ Explain the difference between the mercy seat of the temple and the one in heaven? What did Jesus do?

_____

_____

_____

_____

4/ What were the items inside the Ark of the Covenant that have been put to death under the blood of Christ?

_____

_____

_____

5/ Who are the angels sitting on the mercy seat and what are they staring down upon? What does this mean and how does it relate to us?

_____

_____

_____

_____

6/ What do we have to pass through to get to the tree of life? How does this relate to the keys of the kingdom?

_____

_____

_____

7/ What's the difference between Abel's blood and Jesus' blood?

_____

_____

_____

_____

REFLECT AND DISCUSS

8/ Jesus' blood is constantly speaking mercy and grace over you. What does this mean to your every day life? How does it change the way you think about the times you find yourself walking according to the flesh? Remember, walking according to the flesh is not doing sins, but walking in your own strength (see p48).

_____

_____

_____

_____

_____

_____

_____

C. THE THRONE

There was no chair in the temple. The priests could never sit down because their work of sacrificing and carrying out ordinances was never finished. The blood of the Old Covenant sacrifices made Israel sin-free only for a year (Hebrews 10:1-4).

> For the law, having a shadow of the good things to come, and not the very image of the things, can never with these same sacrifices, **which they offer continually year by year,** make those who approach perfect. For then would they not have ceased to be offered? For the worshipers, once purified, would have had no more consciousness of sins. But in those sacrifices there is a reminder of sins every year. For it is not possible that the blood of bulls and goats could take away sins.
> **HEBREWS 10:1-4**

But after Jesus sprinkled His blood on the mercy seat, He went to the Father's right hand and **sat down** at the Throne—**the Finished Work was finished, once and for all** (Hebrews 1:3).

> who being the brightness of His glory and the express image of His person, and upholding all things by the word of His power, **when He had by Himself purged our sins, sat down at the right hand of the Majesty on high,** HEBREWS 1:3

◖ There is no more work to be done. The Word is forever settled in

> Also there were many priests, because they were prevented by death from continuing. But He, **because He continues forever, has an unchangeable priesthood.** Therefore He is also able to save to the uttermost those who come to God through Him, since **He always lives to make intercession for them**. For such a High Priest was fitting for us, who is holy, harmless, undefiled, separate from sinners, and has become higher than the heavens; who does not need daily, as those high priests, to offer up sacrifices, first for His own sins and then for the people's, for this He did once for all when He offered up Himself. For the law appoints as high priests men who have weakness, **but the word of the oath, which came after the law, appoints the Son who has been perfected forever.** HEBREWS 7:23-28

heaven (Psalm 119:89). His blood forever proclaims our liberty from hell, sin and death. He is our *eternal* High Priest who is forever interceding for the saints (Hebrews 7:23-28).

> Forever, O LORD,
> Your word is settled in
> heaven. **PSALM 119:89**

He took us with Him, from absolute condemnation to justification, all the way from the Cross to the Throne.

Now we are seated together **with Him** at the right hand of the Father, far above all principality and power in this age or any to come (Ephesians 2:6).

> and raised us up together,
> and made us sit together in
> the heavenly places in Christ
> Jesus, **EPHESIANS 2:6**

This is the Finished Work of Christ
that destroyed every evil work of the devil for all eternity!

ABSORBING DEEPER

1/ Why was there no chair in the temple?

_____

_____

_____

2/ What did Jesus do after He sprinkled His blood on the mercy seat and what is the significance?

_____

_____

_____

3/ What does Jesus' blood proclaim?

_____

_____

REFLECT AND DISCUSS

4/ Where are you seated right now? How should this change how you walk out your life in accordance with the Finished Work of Christ? Refer to Hebrews 4:14-16.

_____

_____

_____

_____

_____

_____

_____

CHAPTER ELEVEN

LIFE IN THE NEW COVENANT

> Therefore, brethren, having boldness to enter the Holiest by the blood of Jesus, by a new and living way which He consecrated for us, through the veil, that is, His flesh, and having a High Priest over the house of God, let us draw near with a true heart in full assurance of faith, **_having our hearts sprinkled from an evil conscience_** and our bodies washed with pure water. HEBREWS 10:19-22

We're not supposed to be sin conscious in the New Covenant. Looking over our shoulder, self-chastising and continually confessing sins, we will cause ourselves to sin even more (Romans 5:20-21). **_If we do sin, we have an advocate with the Father_** (1 John 2:1). We have not distanced ourselves from God and He does not withhold any blessings of provision. He is faithful, even when we are not (2 Timothy 2:13).

Our Christian walk is not about trying to control our behavior in order to be good, moral people —this is good and evil thinking. If we think that's what life in Christ is about **_our whole understanding of the gospel is incorrect._**

Once we are washed by the

> Moreover **_the law entered that the offense might abound_**. But where sin abounded, **_grace abounded much more_**, so that as sin reigned in death, even so grace might reign through righteousness to eternal life through Jesus Christ our Lord. ROMANS 5:20-21
>
> My little children, these things I write to you, so that you may not sin. **_And if anyone sins, we have an Advocate with the Father_**, Jesus Christ the righteous. 1 JOHN 2:1
>
> If we are faithless, He remains faithful; He cannot deny Himself. 2 TIMOTHY 2:13

blood of Christ, our relationship is restored *eternally* and we have been justified *eternally*, regardless of our behavior. It's the influence of His Spirit that *causes us* to bear the fruit of the Spirit. Our job is to simply yield to His leading.

NO LAW, NO SIN

Since we are not under the law in Christ, **there is no sin**[1] (Romans 4:15). We are not under the law's jurisdiction any more—it doesn't even apply to us (Romans 10:4). Instead, it's been established in our heart and put in our mind (Ezekiel 36:26-27).

> because the law brings about wrath; for where there is no law **there is no transgression.**[1] **ROMANS 4:15**
>
> For Christ is the end of the law for righteousness to everyone who believes. **ROMANS 10:4**
>
> **I will give you a new heart and put a new spirit within you**; I will take the heart of stone out of your flesh and give you a heart of flesh. **I will put My Spirit within you and cause you to walk** in My statutes, and you will keep My judgments and do them. **EZEKIEL 36:26-27**

God's repetition of this phrase throughout the Old Testament conveys His longing desire for the New Creation man who would follow Him willingly and do righteousness by his very nature. **Now this nature is a reality.** Learning to walk according to the Spirit, following the leading of our New Creation heart, we'll automatically produce fruit of the Spirit (Galatians 5:22-23). Just like a fruit tree produces fruit according to its kind, so will we. Our redeemed spirit man will become dominant and the voice of the flesh will fade.

> But the fruit of the Spirit is love, joy, peace, longsuffering, kindness, goodness, faithfulness, gentleness, self-control. Against such there is no law. **GALATIANS 5:22-23**
>
> For we are His workmanship, created in Christ Jesus for good works, which God prepared beforehand that we should walk in them. **EPHESIANS 2:10**

In the New Covenant, not only are we eternally justified and restored to relationship, but being created in Christ, good works are simply a result of His growing influence on our life (Ephesians 2:10). For example, our parent/child relationship with our children never changes by their behavior—we are eternally their parent, they are eternally our child. But our fellowship relationship, or lack thereof, directly influences their behavior.

OUR JUSTIFICATION IS ETERNAL

🜄 We'll never comprehend our eternal justification until we understand we can't be justified by the law, or try to better ourselves by it. We can't *begin in the Spirit and then go on to be made perfect by the flesh*. One of the sharpest rebukes of the New Testament, Paul called this utter *foolishness* (Galatians 3:1-3).

The whole purpose of the law was to show us our sin nature and that we need His solution (Romans 3:19-20, Chapter 4). The law's continued purpose is to convict the world of the same in the hope every man would willingly come and receive His eternal justification through Christ.

> *O foolish Galatians!* Who has bewitched you that you should not obey the truth, before whose eyes Jesus Christ was clearly portrayed among you as crucified? This only I want to learn from you: Did you receive the Spirit by the works of the law, or by the hearing of faith? Are you so foolish? *Having begun in the Spirit, are you now being made perfect by the flesh?* GALATIANS 3:1-3
>
> Now we know that whatever the law says, it says to those who are under the law, *that every mouth may be stopped, and all the world may become guilty before God. Therefore by the deeds of the law no flesh will be justified in His sight, for by the law is the knowledge of sin.* ROMANS 3:19-20

THE SUPERNATURAL LIFE

By believing in Jesus and receiving by faith what He did on our behalf we take part in the trinity:

1. We are cleansed by the blood of *Jesus.*

2. We are restored to peace with *God the Father.*

3. We qualify to receive the *Holy Spirit*, the miracle-working power of God who is at work in the earth today.

In restored, revelation relationship, this is where the Spirit-empowered life of the believer *begins*.

Having escaped the corruption in the world, even the corruption that exists in our flesh, we are *partakers of the divine nature right now* (2 Peter 1:4). Yes, the fullness of the divine nature is in the future, but in the New Creation, we have a *large down-payment[2] of the future promise right now* (Ephesians 1:13-14).

KEY GREEK WORD

728 ARRABÓN:[2] (ar-hrab-ohn') an earnest (a part payment in advance for security), *a large part of the payment, given in advance as a security that the whole will be paid afterwards.*

by which have been given to us exceedingly great and precious promises, *that through these you may be partakers of the divine nature,* having escaped the corruption that is in the world through lust. **2 PETER 1:4**

In Him you also trusted, after you heard the word of truth, the gospel of your salvation; in whom also, having believed, you were sealed with the Holy Spirit of promise, who is the *guarantee[2]* of our inheritance until the redemption of the purchased possession, to the praise of His glory. **EPHESIANS 1:13-14**

Just like they knew *God was with Him[3]* by the supernatural signs Jesus did (John 3:2-3), the unsaved world around us should know that we walk with God, not only by the natural outpouring of His love displayed in our New Creation heart (John 13:34-35), but by the same supernatural evidence that Jesus displayed. He said that every

This man came to Jesus by night and said to Him, "Rabbi, we know that You are a teacher come from God; *for no one can do these signs that You do unless God is with him."[3]* Jesus answered and said to him, "Most assuredly, I say to you, unless one is born again, he cannot see the kingdom of God." **JOHN 3:2-3**

A new commandment I give to you, that you love one another; as I have loved you, that you also love one another. *By this all will know that you are My disciples, if you have love for one another."* **JOHN 13:34-35**

believer[4] would have signs following (Mark 16:17) and all who *believe*[4] on Him will do the works He did, and *greater*[5] (John 14:12). Through developing our revelation relationship with the Holy Spirit, *believing*[4] and walking in the *greater works*[5] will

> And *these signs will follow those who believe:*[4] In My name they will cast out demons; they will speak with new tongues; they will take up serpents; and if they drink anything deadly, it will by no means hurt them; they will lay hands on the sick, and they will recover." **MARK 16:17**
>
> "Most assuredly, I say to you, he who *believes*[4] in Me, the works that I do he will do also; and *greater works*[5] than these he will do, because I go to My Father. **JOHN 14:12**

become automatic. We will witness to Him, and be evidence of His victory that took place between the Cross and the Throne!

CORRECTLY DISCERNING THE WORD OF TRUTH

> But to him who does not work but believes on Him who justifies the ungodly, his faith is accounted for righteousness, **ROMANS 4:5**
>
> Therefore, having been justified by faith, we have peace with God through our Lord Jesus Christ, **ROMANS 5:1**
>
> There is therefore no condemnation to those who are in Christ Jesus, who do not walk according to the flesh, but according to the Spirit. **ROMANS 8:1**

With the correct understanding of the Finished Work of Christ and the New Creation man through Romans 4:5, 5:1 and 8:1, we will correctly understand the whole Bible.

Never looking at our own efforts, always totally dependent on Him, we find true liberty. We effortlessly stand in faith knowing that the Finished Work provided everything for us. We never have to fear condemnation because we understand our eternal justification. We'll automatically produce good fruit and manifest the kingdom of God on earth.

ABSORBING DEEPER

1/ What does it mean to have our hearts sprinkled from an evil conscience? Hebrews 10:19-22

_____

_____

_____

2/ Rather than controlling our behavior by trying to keep the law, what is the New Covenant way of producing the fruit of the Spirit?

_____

_____

_____

3/ In your own words, what does 2 Peter 1:4 say? How is it possible to take part in the divine nature now?

_____

_____

_____

4/ How will the world know we walk with God?

_____

_____

5/ What did Jesus emphatically assure us of in John 14:12?

_____

_____

_____

_____

_____

REFLECT AND DISCUSS

6/ Meditate on Romans 4:5, 5:1 and 8:1. Write a one sentence explanation of each scripture as it relates to you.

_____

_____

_____

_____

_____

_____

_____

7/ Describe how you expect to walk in true liberty, experience effortless faith, and produce the fruit of the Spirit. What new understanding do you have?

_____

_____

_____

_____

_____

_____

_____

_____

_____

CHAPTER TWELVE

The Age of Rest

> For **he who has entered His rest[1] has himself also ceased from his works** as God did from His. **HEBREWS 4:10**

The picture of God completing all His work on the sixth day, then resting on the seventh, is the shadow of the true **Rest of God.[1]**

When Christ completed the Finished Work and sat down at the right hand of the Father, the age of **Rest[1]** began. This "seventh day of creation" is also known as the age of grace, the Church age, the Sabbath Rest, and the year of Jubilee.

Throughout scripture, God has used many shadows and types about **rest[1]** to train all of us, not just the Israelites. These pictures were designed to **open the eyes of our understanding to trust and submit to His leadership,[3] and rest[1] in His promises of supernatural provision.[2]** Let's look at a few here.

> Then the Lord said to Moses, "Behold, I will rain bread from heaven for you. And the people shall go out and **gather a certain quota every day,[2] that I may test them, whether they will walk in My law[3] or not.** And it shall be on the sixth day that they shall prepare what they bring in, and **it shall be twice as much[2]** as they gather daily." **EXODUS 16:4-5**
>
> And Moses said to them, "This is the bread which the Lord **has given you to eat.[2] EXODUS 16:15**

> And Moses said, "Let no one leave any of it till morning." Notwithstanding they did not heed Moses. But some of them left part of it until morning, and it bred worms and stank. And Moses was angry with them. So they gathered it every morning, every man according to his need. And when the sun became hot, it melted. **EXODUS 16:19-21**
>
> And so it was, on the sixth day, that they gathered twice as much **bread,²** two omers for each one. And all the rulers of the congregation came and told Moses. Then he said to them, "This is what the Lord has said: *'Tomorrow is a Sabbath rest,¹ a holy Sabbath to the Lord.* Bake what you will bake today, and boil what you will boil; and lay up for yourselves all that remains, to be kept until morning.' " So they laid it up till morning, as Moses commanded; and it did not stink, nor were there any worms in it. Then Moses said, "Eat that today, for today is a Sabbath to the Lord; today you will not find it in the field. Six days you shall gather it, but on the seventh day, the Sabbath, there will be none." **EXODUS 16:22-26**

❶ When the Israelites were in the wilderness, God introduced the Sabbath day of *rest¹* (Exodus 16). God's **supernatural provision of manna,²** a shadow of the true bread of life (Chapter 10, p89-91), rained down from heaven every night to be gathered in the morning. There was enough for them to be fully satisfied each day and they were to gather no more than the need for the day. On the sixth day they were instructed to gather twice as much. Then on the Sabbath, **they were commanded³ to rest¹** from their work and eat from the **extra provision²** of the day before.

Later in Leviticus, amongst all the ordinances of the Old Covenant, the seventh year was declared to be a year of rest—*the Sabbath Rest.¹* God **commanded³** that the land was not to be worked or harvested for a whole year—no works of the hand (Leviticus 25:2-4). Instead of

> **"Speak³** to the children of Israel, and say to them: 'When you come into the land which I give you, then the land **shall keep a sabbath to the Lord.** Six years you shall sow your field, and six years you shall prune your vineyard, and gather its fruit; but **in the seventh year there shall be a sabbath of solemn rest¹ for the land,** a sabbath to the Lord. You shall neither sow your field nor prune your vineyard. **LEVITICUS 25:2-4**

> And you shall consecrate the fiftieth year, and *proclaim liberty*[4] throughout all the land to all its inhabitants. It shall be a *Jubilee*[4] for you; and each of you shall return to his possession, and each of you shall return to his family. **LEVITICUS 25:10**
>
> 'So you shall *observe My statutes and keep My judgments,*[3] and perform them; and you will dwell in the land in safety. Then *the land will yield its fruit,*[2] and you will eat your fill, and dwell there in safety. **LEVITICUS 25:18-19**
>
> "At the end of every seven years *you shall grant a release of debts.*[4] And this is the form of the release: Every creditor who has lent anything to his neighbor shall release it; he shall not require it of his neighbor or his brother, because it is called the Lord's release. **DEUTERONOMY 15:1-2**

working to provide for themselves, *by faith,*[6] they had to *trust in God's instructions and promises of provision*[2] (Leviticus 25:18-19).

In Deuteronomy 15:1-2, God declared all debts were to be *completely wiped away*[4]—a picture of *grace.*[5]

The *year of Jubilee*[4] was declared in the fiftieth year. Added onto the Sabbath Rest instructions, slaves were to be *set free.*[4] (Leviticus 25:10).

WALKING IN THE SUBSTANCE OF THE PICTURE

All these things are a picture of the *rest*[1] *of the New Covenant;* we have been *set free*[4] from the law (Chapter 4 and Galatians 5:1) and all of *our debt from sin has been forgiven*[4] (Ephesians 1:7). From this position of *grace,*[5] we rest in *His provision*[2] *and leadership*[3] and carry out our lives in the *substance* of these Old Testament pictures.

> Stand fast therefore in the *liberty*[4] by which Christ has made us free, and do not be entangled again with a yoke of bondage. **GALATIANS 5:1**
>
> In Him we have redemption through His blood, the forgiveness of sins, according to the riches of His grace **EPHESIANS 1:7**

In contrast, the Israelites couldn't enter into the promised land (the *Rest*[1] of God) because they *continually doubted*[6] God's *leadership*[3]

> Now with whom was He angry forty years? Was it not with those who sinned, whose corpses fell in the wilderness? And to whom did He swear that they would not enter His rest, but to those who did not obey? So we see that **they could not enter in because of unbelief.**[6] **HEBREWS 3:17-19**
>
> Therefore, since a promise remains of entering His rest, let us fear lest any of you seem to have come short of it. For indeed the gospel was preached to us as well as to them; **but the word which they heard did not profit them, not being mixed with faith**[7] **in those who heard it. HEBREWS 4:1-2**

and promises of provision.[2] It wasn't their sin God was angry at. It was their **unbelief**[6] (Hebrews 3:17-19)!

His beloved chosen people that He freed from slavery would not simply trust and **believe Him.**[7] Not even after so many miraculous demonstrations of His mercy and grace (Hebrews 4:1-2).

ENTERING INTO HIS REST BY FAITH

Now we enter into His **Rest**[1] by **faith**[7] in the Finished Work. In Christ, **all our debt from the condemnation of sin has been wiped out.**[4] We have ceased from works to be right in God's eyes, and ceased from self-effort to provide for ourselves—we **rest**[1] in His **provision.**[2]

In Luke 4:18-19, Jesus stood in the temple and declared the fulfillment of the prophecy about Himself in Isaiah 61—Jesus, the Anointed One, released us into this **liberty.**[4] His death, burial and resurrection proclaims **the acceptable year of the Lord**[4]**—the year of Jubilee.**[4]

> "The Spirit of the Lord is upon Me, because He has anointed Me to preach the gospel to the poor; He has sent Me to heal the brokenhearted, **to proclaim liberty**[4] **to the captives** and recovery of sight to the blind, to set at **liberty**[4] those who are oppressed; **To proclaim the acceptable year of the Lord.**"[3] **LUKE 4:18-19**

Of course, ceasing from work doesn't mean we quit our jobs and stop doing the work required for every day life. ⬤ The difference is, we do everything in relationship with God the

> He who did not spare His own Son, but delivered Him up for us all, how shall He not with Him also *freely give us all things?²*
> **ROMANS 8:32**
>
> Trust in the Lord with all thine heart; *and lean not unto thine own understanding.* In all thy ways acknowledge him, and *he shall direct thy paths.⁷*
> **PROVERBS 3:5-6**
>
> *looking unto Jesus, the author and finisher of our faith,⁷* who for the joy that was set before Him endured the cross, despising the shame, and has sat down at the right hand of the throne of God. **HEBREWS 12:2**

Father through the Holy Spirit in *faith⁷* of all He *provided²* (Romans 8:32). Instead of *leaning to our own understanding* and the arm of our flesh, we do everything *looking unto Jesus,* the author and finisher of our *faith⁷* (Proverbs 3:5-6, Hebrews 12:2). Our level of *submission to His leadership³* will determine how much of the power of God is operating in our lives.

We must get our head around this—our old nature wants to do everything of ourselves. Without submitting to the renewal of our mind in relationship with Him, we'll keep drifting into self effort. Powerless, never consistently walking in *grace,⁵* we'll continue to get the results of the cursed earth and flesh. We'll be just like the Israelites who wandered the wilderness their whole lives and never entered into their Promised Land.

GOD DID ALL THE WORK FOR US:

He provided the spotless lamb.

He gave us His gift of righteousness.

He justified us eternally.

He gave us a new nature.

He restored us to personal and intimate relationship.

He bound Himself to us in covenant to bless us eternally.

He filled us with His Holy Spirit to forever empower our walk.

He blessed us with every spiritual blessing in the heavenlies.

He seated us next to Him in Christ.

From condemnation to death, to eternal blessing and life, He is the one who has stooped down to our level to snatch us out of the clutches of death and corruption.

There is nothing more to be done but put down our self effort and receive His amazing gift of righteousness by faith in Christ.

We can't be ignorant of God's righteousness and try to establish our own (Romans 10:1-4). Instead, we are to become skilled in our understanding of the word of righteousness. This is the very foundation of our spiritual maturity (Hebrews 5:13).

> Brethren, my heart's desire and prayer to God for Israel is that they may be saved. For I bear them witness that they have a zeal for God, but not according to knowledge. For *they being ignorant of God's righteousness, and seeking to establish their own righteousness, have not submitted to the righteousness of God.* For Christ is the end of the law for righteousness to everyone who believes. **ROMANS 10:1-4**
>
> For everyone who partakes only of milk is *unskilled in the word of righteousness,* for he is a babe. **HEBREWS 5:13**

FROM CURSED TO SUPERNATURAL

The curse is condemnation unto death, which we were born into.

The blessing is justification by faith, which we have to receive through Christ as a gift, not of ourselves.

The outcome is supernatural empowerment by the Holy Spirit, which we have to learn to walk in the fullness thereof, from now until He returns.

ABSORBING DEEPER

1/ When did the age of rest begin?

_____

_____

2/ According to Hebrews 4:10, what does entering into His rest mean?

_____

_____

3/ What has God been teaching us all through the many pictures of rest throughout scripture?

_____

_____

_____

_____

4/ What (or Who) is manna a picture of?

_____

5/ What did the Israelites have to rely on when they were not allowed to work their land for a whole year?

_____

_____

_____

_____

6/ What is the substance of Jubilee?

_____

_____

REFLECT AND DISCUSS

7/ Why do you think God showed such a clear picture of supernatural provision by manna raining down from heaven, as opposed to natural provisions that came from the earth?

_____

_____

_____

_____

_____

8/ What do you think the limits (or parameters) are on Romans 8:32? Have you had limiting ideas about what He would provide?

_____

_____

_____

_____

_____

9/ How are you more able to walk in the substance of the rest of God now? Think of times you have been an unbelieving Israelite. Think of times you have been as bold as Joshua and Caleb (Read Numbers 13).

_____

_____

_____

_____

_____

10/ The last time you walked in unbelief, what actions and words resulted? Can you see how you automatically reverted to self-reliance?

_____

_____

_____

_____

_____

_____

11/ Recall a testing time that required you to walk by faith. What were the words and actions that automatically sprung forth? Explain how you leaned on God's promises of supernatural provision?

_____

_____

_____

_____

_____

_____

12/ Look at the list on page 149. Think about all the things you need to live victoriously in your life right now. God did not leave anything out. Rewrite this list in the first person making it a personal confession.

_____

_____

_____

_____

_____

CHAPTER THIRTEEN
RECEIVING SALVATION

> that if you confess with your mouth the Lord Jesus
> and believe in your heart that God has raised Him
> from the dead, you will be saved. For with the heart
> one believes unto righteousness, and with the mouth
> confession is made unto salvation. **ROMANS 10:9-10**
>
> If we confess our sins, He is faithful and just to
> forgive us our sins and to cleanse us from all
> unrighteousness. **1 JOHN 1:9**

We cannot reconcile ourselves to God. Every person must see and acknowledge their inability to be right in His eyes. Based on Romans 10:9-10 and 1 John 1:9, it's a simple confession. If we believe in our heart and confess with our mouth, He is faithful to forgive us and we will be saved. Say this simple prayer to receive Him now.

SALVATION PRAYER

God, I can see I'm born of a corrupted sin nature.
I need you to save me from this cursed and hopeless state.
Jesus, I confess you are the Christ, the Son of God.
You took my sentence of death upon yourself.
I believe you were resurrected by the Holy Spirit.
I receive you and the forgiveness of my sin.
Cleanse my heart from all unrighteousness
and fill me with your Holy Spirit. Amen

If you said this prayer from your heart you just received the automatic *indwelling*[10] of the Holy Spirit. Your spirit has been completely reborn. God has taken the stony rebellious heart out and given you the New Creation heart, which has His law written on it. You are a completely new creation in Christ (Chapter 7) and the Spirit-empowered life begins here!

CONNECTING WITH A CHURCH

It's essential to find a spirit-filled, bible-believing church where we can connect with the body of Christ and grow together in Him. The Lord is our Good Shepherd and we are His sheep (John 10:11), and all sheep need an earthly shepherd.

God has designed a system of leadership through the five-fold ministry and His blessings flow through this divine order described in Psalm 133:1-3.

The *oil*[1] is the *anointing*[1] *and blessing*[1] that flows from the head of the church (Jesus), down

> "I am the good shepherd. The good shepherd gives His life for the sheep. **JOHN 10:11**
>
> Behold, how good and how pleasant it is for brethren to dwell together in unity! It is like the precious *oil*[1] upon the **head**, running down on the **beard**, the beard of Aaron, running down on the edge of his **garments**. It is like the dew of Hermon, descending upon the mountains of Zion; *for there the Lord commanded the blessing*[1]— life forevermore. **PSALM 133:1-3**

upon the beard (church leadership), and continues to flow to the garments (the body of Christ). The power of God always flows down through the conduit of His divine order. We become equipped to do the supernatural work of the ministry under the *anointing*[1] as we learn to submit to His ordained leadership and divine order.

And so, by this it's easy to see why it's essential to be led by the Holy Spirit when choosing a church.

NEW TESTAMENT CHURCH ORDER

Ephesians 4 (next page) contains a clear picture of this divine order described in Psalm 133:1-3.

> But to each one of us *grace² was given³* according to the measure of Christ's *gift.⁴* Therefore He says: "When He ascended on high, He led captivity captive, and *gave³ gifts⁴ to men."* **EPHESIANS 4:7-8**

The *grace²* is the supernatural empowerment, or *anointing,¹ given³* to each of us to do ministry. The measure we receive comes down from the *gifts⁴ that Christ gives³*—the five-fold ministry (Ephesians 4:7-8).

> And He Himself *gave³ some⁵* to be apostles, *some⁵* prophets, *some⁵* evangelists, and *some⁵* pastors and teachers, *for the equipping⁶ of the saints for the work of ministry, for the edifying⁷ of the body* of Christ, till we all come to the unity of the faith and of the knowledge of the Son of God, to a perfect man, to the measure of the stature of the fullness of Christ; **EPHESIANS 4:11-13**

Listed here is the five-fold ministry *giftings⁴* that are *given³ to some,⁵ not all.* These ministry offices are appointed for the purpose of *edifying⁷ and equipping⁶ all the saints* to grow into maturity to carry out Spirit-empowered ministry. It's Gods intention that *everyone in the body of Christ* comes to the unity of faith and knowledge of Jesus' Finished Work, rising to the stature of the fullness of Christ (Ephesians 4:11-13). This describes being *equipped⁶* with this supernatural *anointing¹* of *grace²* for our own lives *and* for ministering to others. We receive by cooperating and coming into alignment with the local church under the leadership of the five-fold ministry.

THE TWO ORDINANCES OF THE NEW COVENANT

Ordinances are something God instructed us to do. They are a requirement and a command. In the same way the sacrifices of the temple were a shadow of Jesus' perfect sacrifice, ordinances are actions put in place that are a picture of things to come.

As we carry out an ordinance, we put our faith on the picture and through doing so, we appropriate a portion of the future promise now.

There are two ordinances of the New Covenant—Communion (Chapter 10, p86 and p112) and Baptism.

TWO BAPTISMS

Let's discuss two important baptisms; *water baptism*[8] and the *baptism of the Holy Spirit.*[9]

As clearly described in Acts 8:14-17 and 19:1-6, it is possible to be washed by the blood, water baptized and secure in our eternal justification, but not receive *the baptism of the Holy Spirit.*[9]

> Now when the apostles who were at Jerusalem heard that Samaria had received the word of God, they sent Peter and John to them, who, when they had come down, prayed for them that they might receive the Holy Spirit. *For as yet He had fallen upon*[9] *none of them. They had only been baptized*[8] *in the name of the Lord Jesus. Then they laid hands on them, and they received the Holy Spirit.*[9] ACTS 8:14-17

But it is through the *enduing upon*[9] of the Holy Spirit that we will walk in the *power*[1] that God purposefully intended. This *power*[1] is not just for ourselves, but for witnessing unto His resurrection *to the ends of the earth.*[12]

> And it happened, while Apollos was at Corinth, that Paul, having passed through the upper regions, came to Ephesus. And finding some disciples he said to them, *"Did you receive the Holy Spirit*[9] *when you believed?"* So they said to him, "We have not so much as heard whether there is a Holy Spirit." And he said to them, *"Into what then were you baptized?"* So they said, "Into John's baptism." Then Paul said, "John indeed baptized with a baptism of repentance, saying to the people that they should believe on Him who would come after him, that is, on Christ Jesus." When they heard this, they were baptized in the name of the Lord Jesus. *And when Paul had laid hands on them, the Holy Spirit came upon them,*[9] and they spoke with tongues and prophesied. ACTS 19:1-6

Like Jesus' example when He was *baptized by John*[8] (Chapter 10, Part 1), both baptisms can happen at the same time. But many times, as described in Acts 19:1-6, they can happen at different times.

Either way, it's clear the **baptism of the Holy Spirit**[9] is separate from **water baptism,**[8] and tongues is the evidence of having received (Mark 16:17).

> **"And these signs will accompany those who believe:** in my name they will cast out demons; they will speak in new tongues;…" **MARK 16:17**

WATER BAPTISM

Water baptism[8] is an outward expression of our inward faith. Through this ordinance we are declaring our faith in Jesus' Finished Work to God, to people, and to the devil.

Baptism is a picture of our future resurrection. When we go under the water, we identify with His death and burial. When we come out, we identify with the resurrection.

THE BAPTISM OF THE HOLY SPIRIT

The Baptism of the Holy Spirit[9] is a **command,**[11] not a suggestion. This controversial subject is so significant that it was **the very last instruction** Jesus gave before He ascended, not just to His disciples but to all who were present. Let's take a closer look by understanding the two applications of the Holy Spirit, the **indwelling**[10] and the **enduing upon.**[9]

When Jesus stood among the disciples **on resurrection day,**

> **KEY GREEK WORD**
>
> **1720 EMPHUSAÓ:**[10] (em-foo-sah'-o) **to breathe into** or upon

He re-enacted the moment that God breathed life **into**[10] Adam (Chapter 2). As He breathed **into**[10] them, He released the new birth and said **"Receive the Holy Spirit"** (John 20:22).

> And when He had said this, **He breathed on them,**[10] and said to them, **"Receive the Holy Spirit.** JOHN 20:22

This was the moment the Holy Spirit first came to dwell **on the inside**[10] of the believer. This is equivalent to the automatic **indwelling of the Holy Spirit**[10] that happens when we receive Christ.

> And being assembled together with them, *He commanded[11] them* not to depart from Jerusalem, but to wait for the Promise of the Father, "which," He said, "you have heard from Me; for *John truly baptized with water,[8]* but *you shall be baptized with the Holy Spirit[9]* not many days from now." ACTS 1:4-5
>
> But *you shall receive power[1] when the Holy Spirit has come upon[9] you;* and you shall be witnesses to Me in Jerusalem, and in all Judea and Samaria, and *to the end of the earth."[12]* Now when He had spoken these things, while they watched, He was taken up, and a cloud received Him out of their sight. ACTS 1:8-9

Then in Acts 1:4-5 and 1:8-9, *forty days later on the day of His ascension,* Jesus gave them His very last instruction—*He commanded[11] them* to wait for the *enduing upon[9]* of the Holy Spirit, the *anointing of power[1] from on high.*

Noting the definition of 1746 ENDUO,[9] being *endued[9] with power[1] from on high* (Luke 24:49) is clearly the restoration of the

KEY GREEK WORD

1746 ENDUO:[9] (en-doo'-o) to clothe or be clothed with (in the sense of sinking into a garment)

clothing of glory *upon[9]* the New Covenant saint! Just like Adam was clothed with the glory (Chapter 2), so are we once again.

> Behold, I send the Promise of My Father *upon you;[9]* but tarry in the city of Jerusalem until you are *endued[9] with power[1] from on high." LUKE 24:49*

THE TWO APPLICATIONS OF THE HOLY SPIRIT

The indwelling[10] of the Holy Spirit is an automatic result of being washed in the blood, and proceeds from the new birth.

The enduing upon[9] of the Holy Spirit is something we must actively receive. This *command[11]* that Jesus gave in His last moments before He went to the Father is directed at all of us still today. With it flows the evidence of the heavenly language, the tongues of fire that separate. Study *Speak It:® 30 Days of Saturation in the Spirit-Empowere⚫ Life* for more in depth understanding of this crucial gift for the believer.

THE COMPLETION OF THE HOLY SPIRIT

There is another important connection to recognize in Ephesians 5:18.

Because of our understanding of the English word, *fill,* we typically understand Paul's command to *be filled*[13] akin to being filled up on the inside like a glass of water. But if we look at the definition of 4134 PLÉRÉS[13] we see a more accurate translation —*to be complete.*[13]

> And do not be drunk with wine, in which is dissipation; but *be filled*[13] with the Spirit, **EPHESIANS 5:18**

> **KEY GREEK WORD**
> 4134 PLÉRÉS:[13] (play'-race) full, abounding in, **complete,** completely occupied with.

Clearly, the two applications *together,* the *indwelling*[10] and the *enduing upon,*[9] are the *completion*[13] of the restoration of the Holy Spirit to the believer.

🔑 Now noting the grammar of this word (present tense, imperative mood and active voice) we see Paul is reiterating Jesus' *command*[11] (Acts 1:4-5 previous page) to *be filled,*[13] or rather to *be completed*[13] with the Spirit. Furthermore, the active voice and imperative mood

> For those who live according to the flesh set their minds on the things of the flesh, but those who live according to the Spirit, the things of the Spirit. For to be carnally minded is death, but to be spiritually minded is life and peace. **ROMANS 8:5-6**

strongly emphasizes that *we* must actively, purposefully and continually *submit ourselves* to be in constant fellowship with the Holy Spirit. But rather than tending to work to achieve something in and of ourselves, we give Him permission to do the work in us, and we simply yield to His empowerment. Our prayer language that comes from the *Baptism of the Holy Spirit*[9] helps to keep us spiritually-minded (Romans 8:5-6) and continually growing in our ability to perceive and submit to His leadership (p121-125).

This is a complex and essential subject that is one of the central topics of *Speak It:® 30 Days of Saturation in the Spirit-Empowered Life.*

THE SUBSTANCE OF THE ARK OF THE COVENANT

With both applications of the Holy Spirit, *we are the substance* of the shadow of the Ark of the Covenant.

Made of acacia wood and completely covered on the inside and on the outside with pure gold, the ark was

> Do you not know that you are the temple of God and that the Spirit of God dwells in you? **1 CORINTHIANS 3:16**

the vessel that carried the presence of God. Now we are the temple of God and we carry His presence (1 Corinthians 3:16). Our natural man (represented by the acacia wood) is completely covered by the Holy Spirit (represented by the gold)—the resurrection power *in us*[10] and *on us.*[9]

RECEIVING THE BAPTISM OF THE HOLY SPIRIT

The *Baptism of the Holy Spirit*[9] must be received by faith, typically with the laying on of hands. With the guidance of a mature believer who knows how to minister the gift, all we need is a clear biblical understanding and a desire to receive.

We can take hold of it at the same time as water baptism. As we go down into the water identifying with the death and burial of Christ, we come up out of the water identifying with being raised by the resurrection power right now. We say "I am raised" and accept it is true by faith (Ephesians 2:5-6). We come up speaking by putting sound behind our breath, and allowing the Holy Spirit to fill our tongue. In

> even when we were dead in trespasses, *made us alive together* with Christ (by grace you have been saved), and *raised us up together,* and *made us sit together* in the heavenly places in Christ Jesus, **EPHESIANS 2:5-6**

this act, we are declaring "it's true according to me, it is finished according to me, and now I have the resurrection power of the Holy Spirit in my life."

But if it's not at the moment of water baptism, we can receive the baptism of the Holy Spirit anytime. For further help watch the *Holy Spirit Studio Live* series on *YouTube.com/c/SpeakIt,* or go to *SpeakItPower.com/contact.*

"So I say to you, ask, and it will be given to you; seek, and you will find; knock, and it will be opened to you. For everyone who asks receives, and he who seeks finds, and to him who knocks it will be opened. If a son asks for bread from any father among you, will he give him a stone? Or if he asks for a fish, will he give him a serpent instead of a fish? Or if he asks for an egg, will he offer him a scorpion? If you then, being evil, know how to give good gifts to your children, how much more will your heavenly Father *give the Holy Spirit* to those who ask Him!" **LUKE 11:9-13**

ASK, SEEK, KNOCK

Luke 11:9-13 declares that we will receive His good and precious gift, the *empowerment[1]* of the Holy Spirit, simply by asking. And it's through His *empowerment[1]* that we access all things that He freely gives (Chapter 5).

THE RESURRECTION POWER *IS* THE HOLY SPIRIT

Therefore we were buried with Him through baptism into death, that just as *Christ was raised from the dead by the glory of the Father, even so we also should walk in newness of life.* **ROMANS 6:4**

But if *the Spirit of Him who raised Jesus from the dead* dwells in you, He who raised Christ from the dead will also give life to your mortal bodies through His Spirit who dwells in you. **ROMANS 8:11**

Romans 6:4 declares the glory raised Christ from the dead. Just two chapters later, Romans 8:11 declares that the Spirit raised Jesus from the dead. These two verses just two chapters apart, prove that the glory, the Holy Spirit and the resurrection power *are all one and the same.*

Now the *completion[13]* of the Holy Spirit forever *empowers[1]* our walk. We have been *indwelt[10]* and *clothed upon[9]* by the *glory[1] of God* (Romans 6:4). Jesus was resurrected by the glory, and we have been instructed to walk out our New Creation life *in the same manner* —by the *resurrection power[1]* of God!

ABSORBING DEEPER

1/ According to Romans 10:9-10, there are two requirements to receive salvation. What are they?

_____

_____

2/ What is it that we are believing?

_____

_____

3/ Confessing our sins doesn't mean making a long list. What does every person need to acknowledge before God?

_____

_____

4/ What happens automatically when anyone receives salvation?

_____

_____

5/ Why is it important to find a spirit-filled, bible believing church?

_____

_____

6/ Should every believer be anointed and empowered to do the supernatural work of the ministry, like laying hands on the sick?

_____

7/ Does every believer have a five-fold ministry calling?

_____

8/ Explain the purpose of the five-fold leadership of the church.

_____

_____

_____

_____

9/ What is an ordinance?

_____

10/ What are the two ordinances of the New Covenant?

_____

_____

11/ What are we doing when we carry out an ordinance? What does it do?

_____

_____

_____

_____

12/ What are the two baptisms?

_____

_____

13/ How do we know there are two baptisms? What scripture makes it most clear to you?

_____

_____

_____

_____

14/ What is the evidence of having received?

_____

_____

15/ What are the two different applications of the Holy Spirit?

_____

_____

16/ Can you clearly see the two different applications of the Holy Spirit released at different moments in time? From Jesus releasing the indwelling on resurrection day (John 20:22), to His command to wait for the enduing upon on the day of His ascension, 40 days later (Acts 1:3-4, 8-9). Why do we need both? Explain referring to the full meaning of the Greek word **4134 PLÉRÉS**.

_____

_____

_____

_____

17/ We the substance of which Old Covenant shadow when we receive both applications of the Holy Spirit?

_____

_____

18/ Think about how both applications enable us to be carriers of God's presence. Why do you think this is important?

_____

_____

_____

_____

REFLECT AND DISCUSS

19/You can lead anyone in a prayer like this one on page 153. Meditate on the different parts of the salvation prayer until you really understand the important elements it contains. Then write one in your own words.

_____

_____

_____

_____

_____

20/In what way was Jesus sent to do the work of His ministry? How do we know we have been sent in the same way? HINT: Refer to Chapter 10, Part 1.

_____

_____

_____

_____

_____

21/What is apparent looking at Romans 6:4 and 8:11? How can you walk out New Life in this power? What does this practically mean?

_____

_____

_____

_____

_____

Connect

The Finished Work of Christ is so complete. In it is everything we need to walk out our life in the power and authority of Christ. We have been thoroughly equipped to witness unto Jesus **to the ends of the earth,**[12] and reign in life as we soar above the corruption that is still in the earth and flesh.

Subscribe on **SpeakItPower.com** for free resources and to receive notifications of news and events.

Other titles from *Speak It®* include *30 Days of Saturation in Healing* and *30 Days of Saturation in the Spirit-Empowere‹ Life.*

Watch powerful teaching videos on **YouTube.com/c/SpeakIt**

For questions, reach out at **SpeakItPower.com/contact**

Remember, let your tongue set the course of your life according to the power of the Word of God (James 3:6). Mutter it day and night to make your way prosperous (Joshua 1:8), for God is forever watching over His Word to perform it (Jeremiah 1:12).